Pro

This text evolved out of a discussion ....
Not all of the objections, questions or issues are his: some
originate from other people and some are more generic than
personal. I believe all of them to be important.

The chapter entitled "What is the point of the Church"
is a dialogue between myself and Professor Paul Miller, who
subsequently became a Catholic.

The dialogue "Primon" is based on other discussions which
I have had with Professor Miller. It focuses on the doctrine
of the Incarnation and Redemption or Atonement.

The dialogue "Nyxostates", summaries many conversations
I have had with Abid Siddique, another close friend of mine.
It focuses on the problem of suffering and the issue of human
autonomy or free-will.

I hope that my readers will find this book enlightening
and be motivated to investigate further the Catholic Faith.

For further reading, I recommend:

C.S. Lewis "Mere Christianity."
C.S. Lewis "Miracles."
C.S. Lewis "The Problem of Pain."
F.J. Sheed "Theology for Beginners."
F. Morison "Who moved the Stone?"
R. Knox "In Soft Garments."
P. Davies "God and the New Physics"
P. Davies "The Mind of God"
P. Davies "The Goldilocks Enigma"
S.C. Lovatt "The Good of Being."
S.C. Lovatt "Understanding the PSyChE."

Dances with Doubt

Conversations with

a lapsed Catholic

Stephen C. Lovatt

Dances with Doubt
Conversations with a lapsed Catholic

Copyright © 2017 Stephen C. Lovatt

CreateSpace

Seattle, WA. USA

ISBN-10: 1542383641
ISBN-13: 978-1542383646

Fourth Edition (2018)

http://www.createspace.com

For Philip

The light shines in the darkness
and the darkness
has never comprehended it.

Table of Contents

God is an impersonal force

If pushed, I would say that there is probably an "uncaused first cause" behind the existence of the Universe in which we live; but to make any assertions beyond this seems to me to be like guessing what is behind a closed and locked door which has never been opened.

This is about as far as it is possible to get with the "Cosmological Argument"[1,2] and the renewed (Physics rather than Biology based) "Argument from Design".[3] It is what most Theoretical Cosmologists believe, as is demonstrated by their interest in "Multiverse Theory" and similar explanations for the existence of any-thing at all, and for the fine-tuning of the actual universe as we find it.[4] To get further one either has to understand and accept the Ontological Argument (henceforth designated the OA) or else Revelation. The OA[5] is so very important that I will review it here; but first, I will make some preliminary remarks.

One reason that people find the OA difficult to accept is that at first sight it seems to produce a conclusion from no premises, and this would be ridiculous. In fact it does no such thing. The premises which it relies on are as follows:

1. Logic is to be adhered to, remorselessly.
2. The concept of "value" is somehow valid. This proposition might be backed up in various ways, but the validity of the OA does not obviously depend on which justification is adopted.

---

1 For the Cosmological Argument see page 119ff.
2 For a critique of the Pantheism solution to the Cosmological Argument see page 123ff.
3 For the Argument from Design see page 127ff.
4 GOB p245-246.
   P. Davies "The Goldilocks Enigma" (2006)
5 For more on the Ontological Argument see page 133ff.

3.   It is possible to compare values so as to determine
     which is the greater. In particular, values accumulate:
     so if X has the set of values {A, B, C, D} and Y has the
     set of values {A, B, C, D, E} then Y has a greater value
     that X because it has all the values possessed by X
     and another value besides.
4.   It is valuable to be real as opposed to imaginary.
     This is because "being imaginary" implies a dependence
     on an imagining mind, and so a vulnerability to being
     forgotten; whereas "being real" implies independence,
     autonomy, and no vulnerability to any lapse of attention.

Hence it is possible to avoid the conclusion which the OA obtains
by denying one or more of these premises. One can:

1.   reject Logic,
2.   adopt some variety of Nihilism,
3.   refuse to admit that values can ever be compared, or
4.   deny that it is better to be real than to be imaginary.[6]

To negate the OA it is necessary to deny one or more of these
premises absolutely. This means following through on the denial
in the whole of ones mentality and life systematically, and not just
while considering the OA. Personally I find all of these options
repugnant, which is why I accept the OA for what it seems to be.

  Another reason that people find the OA difficult to accept
is that it seems to prove too much. In particular, it seems to prove
that all manner of things exist, when it is clear that they do not.
On the contrary, the fact that it is obvious that these things do not
exist should alert one to the fact that the OA cannot possibly
prove that they do exist, and that the idea that it does prove their
existence is based on a misunderstanding of the OA. I shall
discuss this further, after I have presented the OA.

  A final reason that people find the OA difficult to accept
is that they misunderstand it as amounting to the proposition:
"the fact that I am able to think about a thing proves that

---

6   This is the basis of Kant's objection to the OA, see page 135ff.

this thing must exist." Now this argument is blatantly silly, and the idea that a person as clever and well educated as Anselm of Canterbury (who seems to have been the first person to write down the OA in any recognisable form)[7] could propose so specious an argument is itself ridiculous.

The OA is subtle, and it is necessary to pay close attention to the terms in which it is set. When one does this, it becomes clear that the OA is quite straight-forward and valid. The truth of its conclusion is then only vulnerable to a denial of one or more of the four premises I have already listed.

As a final preliminary, it is necessary to set out what I call "Lovatt's Lemma."[8] This is: "Any object of thought[9] which might, or might not, be real can certainly be imagined as being purely imaginary – that is, fictitious." This, I contend, is straightforward, obviously true and uncontentious.[10] Its converse is: "Any object of thought which cannot be imagined as being purely imaginary – that is, fictitious – must be real, of absolute necessity."

Now it might seem implausible that there is "any object of thought which cannot be imagined as being purely imaginary";[11] but in fact the OA sets about to show that this is not the case, and in fact that there is a whole set of such objects of thought, of which God is the prime and the exemplar.

---

7   See page 133.
8   A lemma is a pretty obvious and almost trivial theorem. The reason that I call this lemma after myself is that to the best of my knowledge it is not generally enunciated, being taken for granted as too obvious to bother stating.
9   Avoiding the word "thing". I use "thing" to mean "a material object."
10 As an illustration, consider "a purple unicorn". Such an animal has never existed on Earth, so far as we know; but it is conceivable that it might exist somewhere in the universe now (or even on the Earth in the future) either as a result of evolutionary change or else human genetic engineering. The fact that "a purple unicorn" involves no absurdities (being only a minor variation on a horse, involving a nasal horn like that of a hippopotamus and a specific dermal hue) means that it is certainly conceivable. The fact that it has never been real, as far as we know (and may or may not ever be real) means that we are free to think of it as never and nowhere having any reality.
11 This is the basis of Hume's objection to the OA, see page 137ff.

Now for the OA itself. Consider the Greatest Conceivable Being – henceforth designated the GCB. The GCB is not the greatest[12] being of which you (or any human being) can conceive, but the greatest being of which any possible conceiver could conceive.[13]

It is certain that the GCB at least *might* be real,[14] and so can be conceived of as being real; for the fact that it is actually conceivable (remember we are considering the Greatest *Conceivable* Being) means that it involves no absurdities or inconsistencies. The only reason that the GCB might not be real is the failure or absence of some precondition or context upon which the reality of the GCB is contingent.

Now, attempt to consider the *exactly similar* object of thought as being purely imaginary: that is, as being entirely dependent for its subsistence[14] on whatever mind, other than itself, which happens to be conceiving it. It is immediately apparent that this latter conception of the GCB – as being purely imaginary, or fictional – is deficient when compared with the former,[15] and hence that the latter conception of the GCB was not in fact the GCB at all, but a mistake.

This means that it is impossible to conceive of the GCB as unreal, but only imaginary: because for the GCB not to be real would be for it to be lack the value of "being real", and so this supposed GCB would not in fact be the *Greatest* Conceivable Being – which is a direct contradiction of specification, and is absurd. Hence, the mere idea of the GCB itself inexorably involves the idea that the GCB is real, and the GCB cannot possibly be conceived of as being only imaginary. Therefore,[16] by Lovatt's Lemma, the GCB must be real of absolute necessity.

---

12 The most "valuable", premise #2 and premise #3.

13 It will turn out that only the GCB can properly conceive of the GCB, but this fact plays no part in the OA.

14 I use the word "subsistence" to mean any mode of being. I reserve "existence" to mean "physical or material subsistence" and "real" to mean "objective autonomous subsistence, independent of any second party, and in particular of an imagining mind."

15 Premise #3 and premise #4.

16 Premise #1.

The OA demonstrates that there is an object of thought[9] which is necessarily real, and that this object of thought is the GCB. It is convenient to designate the GCB by the alternate name "God", as it is clear that the GCB fulfils every criterion by which God might be identified as being God. The OA also demonstrates that every specific perfection (such as "The Perfect Triangle") is real. This is inevitable, because the GCB must encompass every particular perfection in order to be the GCB; hence the reality of every specific perfection is an aspect of the entire reality of the GCB.

Crucially, the OA implies the reality and central importance of the Platonic form of Justice. This is because Platonic Justice is "that state of affairs in which each constituent of a system (such as a human being living in society) is able to fulfil and completely express itself (without any limit, hindrance, or interference) in peace and harmony with every other constituent."[17] It should be apparent that this is the state of affairs which is constitutional of the GCB: which must encompass, incorporate and reconcile every possible perfection within itself.

This means that the foundational perfection which organises all the other perfections within (and so which is constitutional of) the GCB is the Platonic form of Justice, and that this form has its reality within the GCB precisely as the fact that all the other perfections are so organised. From this understanding of the GCB – or "the divine nature", if you prefer – any number of conclusions follow; for if God's fundamental nature is Justice than the ideas of God being Lawful, Peaceful and Benevolent – in an impersonal way – follow close behind.

The OA does not demonstrate that the perfect triangle "exists", as opposed to the perfect triangle "being real". The distinction between "existing" and "being real" is simple. By "exists" I mean "has *physical* subsistence, being constituted of *mass-energy*, at a location in *space-time*." By "being real" I mean having any kind of autonomous subsistence whatsoever – including the kind of subsistence which an idea has in the mind

---

17 Is 11:1-9. 1Cor 12:20-25.
    Plato "Republic" 4:433a

of a thinker.[18] The fact that we are familiar with two kinds of subsistence – mental and physical – does not mean that these are the only two modes of subsistence. This may be the case, but it may not be.

As it happens, it is unnecessary to hypothesis any other kind of subsistence to accommodate the OA. The *non-existent* mode of subsistence of the GCB (and of "The Perfect Triangle", and of "The State of Justice") can be speculatively identified as "being conceived of in the Mind of God". In this case, "being real" is closer to "being imaginary" than one might have thought when rehearsing the OA; for "reality" would then be nothing other than "the imaginings of God". This does not compromise the OA; for the GCB is still entirely autonomous and independent of any object of thought other than the GCB, and is not vulnerable to being forgotten. The GCB is, on this account, the "unimagined self-imaginer."

As for God being "personal" and/or "conscious", which was the question which elicited this response, one must be wary of projecting onto God what it is to be human; so what it might mean for God to be "personal" can be expected to be very different from what it is for a human being to be "personal".[19] Nevertheless, in as far as "being a person" is valuable or a perfection of being (which I strongly suspect to be the case) then God must be "personal" in some analogous and congruent manner, for else the GCB would lack a perfection: which is absurd. Similarly, if "relationship", "community" (and "love" or "friendship" understood as interpersonal bonding) are valuable and/or perfections of being, then the GCB must somehow encompass these realities also.

---

18 Although the idea only temporarily subsists within the mind which thinks it while it is being thought, it does actually subsist there – though fleetingly. Even the idea of a "flying spaghetti monster" has an objective existence, as an idea, while it is been thought; though no actual "flying spaghetti monster" has ever existed, or will ever exist. Hence the idea of the "flying spaghetti monster" is a real idea, even though the "flying spaghetti monster" is itself imaginary – and, I would argue, inconceivable.

19 UPSY

It is significant that the conclusion of the OA (and its set of corollaries) aligns closely with what is revealed in the Bible, where God is portrayed as Absolute Being,[20] Merciful,[21] Benevolent,[22] Omnipotent,[23] and Omniscient.[24] All of these attributes can best be understood as aspects or implications of Substantial Justice.[25] Moreover, in the New Testament it is also revealed that God is a tri-personal community of love.[26]

The Ontological Argument still seems to me to be more about word juggling than anything solid. I don't see how a perfect triangle can be real either. Imaginary and real seem to become the same thing. Your solution to this is that we are all imaginary in the mind of God. This seems to me to be quite a leap, rather than saying that real should be quite different to imagination.

The OA is not "word juggling". It is a syllogism. Syllogisms always seem to be "word jugging" to those not used to abstract logical reasoning. There are only two admissible objections to any argument: it must either be shown that the argument is invalid, or else an objection must be made to one or more of its premises.[27]

---

20 Ex 3:14.
21 Ex 20:6; 33:19; 34:7. Num 14:18-19. Deut 7:9. 1Kgs 8:23. 1Chr 16:34, 41. Ps 22:6; 24:10; 35:5; 56:10; 61:12; 85:5,13,15; 88:2,14; 99:5; 102:8,11,17; 129:7. Is 54:8-10. Hos 6:6. Mic 6:8; 7:18.
22 Ps 17:7; 25:3; 35:7,10; 62:3; 91:2; 106:43. Jer 9:24; 31:3; 32:18. Wis 11:24-26.
23 Job 37:23; 42:2. Wis 11:17,23; 18:15. Apoc 1:8; 11:17; 19:6.
24 Job 21:22; 36:1-9; 37:16. Ps 93:10. Pr 2:6. Is 40:14. Dan 1:17; 2:21. 1Jn 3:20.
25 Gen 18:25. Deut 33:21. Job 8:3; 37:23. Ps 88:14. Prov 21:3. Is 9:7; 56:1. Mic 6:8.
26 Mt 28:19. Lk 4:1; 11:13. Jn 7:39; 10:30; 17:22. Acts 2:4. 1Cor 12:3. Eph 3:5; 4:30. 1Thes 4:8.
27 An argument may rely on an unspoken assumption. In which case this premise should certainly be made explicit. Once this is done, an objection may be made to this newly disclosed premise.

An emotional reaction to, or informal evaluation of, an argument's conclusion or form is no basis for rejecting it.

An imaginary object of thought[9] entirely relies for its subsistence on the fact that it is being thought about by a thinker other than itself: hence it is liable to be forgotten, and in being forgotten of ceasing to subsist at all. Being imaginary involves a vulnerability: dependence or contingency.

A real object of thought[9] has no such vulnerability. Its subsistence is objective. It has autonomy, independence, self-adequacy: it stands alone. While it is being thought about, there is an image of itself in whatever mind might be contemplating it. When this mind ceases to give it attention this image dissipates; but the real object itself is wholly unaffected by this lapse of attention, not itself being imaginary.

Imaginary objects of thought are subjective images which have no correspondence to objective reality. They are no more than fictions; though such fictions may be entertaining, and even useful on occasion. It is not at all the case that "real" and "imaginary" objects of thought are the same. They are fundamentally different. They are differentiated by the former having a vulnerability from which the latter is free.

The idea that real objects of thought are in fact the imaginations of God is only a hypothesis, and plays no part in the OA. It is an elegant hypothesis, nevertheless, with much to commend it once (but only once) one has accepted the conclusion which the OA establishes. Hypothesising real objects of thought to be the imaginings of God does not detract from their objective nature, or render them vulnerable to being forgotten. God is outside time and omniscient. God is incapable of forgetfulness; hence to be an idea in the mind of God is to be almost as absolutely subsistent as God.

Why believe that God is benevolent?

What is the difference on the one hand between me creating a being capable of suffering and then abandoning it to a miserable fate; or else experimenting on it, or torturing it, for some reason unknown – and perhaps incomprehensible – to it, and on the other hand, how God seems to be treating the world which you claim is a divine creation?

What are the options, assuming that God is real?

1. God is benevolent: standard Monotheism.
2. God is indifferent: Deism.
3. God is malevolent: Satanism.

The basic argument I shall propose here is that the second and third options are inadmissible as being incoherent; but this requires development, of course. The underlying issue at stake is the qualitative relationship existing between God-as-God and the physical world which it is supposed that God created. Once more there are a number of obvious options:

1. The Cosmos is (quasi-)identical with God: Pantheism.
2. The Cosmos is, in some way, the natural offspring of God: Generism.
3. The Cosmos is an inevitable consequence of God-being-God: Necessaritism.
4. The Cosmos is the deliberate act of God: Deliberatism.
5. The Cosmos is some kind of accident, side effect, or excrescence of God: Unintentialism.

The first two possibilities (which I reject on philosophical and empirical grounds) both tend to the idea that God is benevolent, as every part of the Cosmos would then be consubstantial with God (that is, fully share the divine nature: not by analogy, or in limited participation, but entirely) and it would be incoherent for God to act in any way that was contrary to God's own interest. I admit that the interest of the whole is not the same as the interest of any one part of the whole (trees shed their leaves; skin cells are programmed to die, so as to become epithelium; and worker bees instinctively commit suicide when they sting any animal that attempts to raid their hive) but the raw fact of consciousness suggests that human beings have a greater significance than tree-leaves, skin-cells and worker-bees.

The third possibility (which I favour, on philosophical grounds) also tends to the idea that God is benevolent. This is because although the Cosmos is then not consubstantial with God, nevertheless it is bound-up with God, absolutely. The best analogy I can propose is the way in which the thoughts of a mind (while not identical with the mind which is doing the thinking of them) are the very purpose, rational and justification of the thinking mind. Similarly, while God is not identical with the Cosmos (as Pantheism proposes) a large part – perhaps the entirety! – of God's business may well be the creation *and perfection* of the Cosmos: and in particular those sapient and conscious beings which inhabit it.

The fourth possibility (this is the conventional Judeo-Christian view, but I think that it is doubtful on philosophical grounds) is vulnerable to to the Calvinist idea that God has made the world so as to exemplify, show-off, demonstrate, exercise and express the divine nature; and part of this nature is "justice", which is understood in terms of "retribution" and "vengeance".

This being the case, it is necessary that there exist injustices to be punished. Therefore suffering is necessary, both as an evil to be punished and as a means of punishment. Hence God acts malevolently, via secondary agents, so as to cause injustice. Of course, there is no need to adopt the Calvinist view of divine retribution; and if one does not do so, it is still possible to believe that God is benevolent; but on less sure grounds than is the case for the first three possibilities: because the motive for God's choice to create the Cosmos will always be a matter of speculation.

The fifth possibility would strongly suggest that God is not benevolent: the Cosmos being spurious and unworthy of notice. It seems to me that Unintentialism. and Deism are two names for the same hypothesis, viewed from differing perspectives. Suffering is then easily explained as the incoherence inevitable in any more or less arbitrary ramshackle contrivance. Against this hypothesis are ranged the stark facts of the fundamental coherence of physical reality – the simplicity and beauty of the laws of physics – and the transcendence of consciousness. These two considerations alone call into serious question the idea that the Cosmos is some kind of spurious occurrence: why should an "accident" have so much about it that looks like anything but an accident?

I will now muster the philosophical and empirical arguments in favour of divine benevolence.

The character of physical law.

The fact that physics is as it is – lawful, neat and tidy – gives ground for hope. Certainly, the Cosmos is not some kind of Tom-and-Jerry nightmare of a place. The Cosmos makes sense at a deep level, and can be understood by the human mind. The Cosmos conforms to mathematical patterns and principles. It is characterised by what the Greeks termed Logos.

The fact of life.

Life – persistence arising out of flux – could be conceived of as a possibility (by a non-living mind) apart from any actual example of a living being. Of course there are actual living organisms. Hence the Cosmos is known to be apt for life as an empirical fact; whereas there is no reason at all why it must be so. The actual existence of life, with its approximation of permanence, suggests the real possibility of absolute eternity. Life is certainly the *ontological basis of value*, worth and so of ethics: apart from life these concepts do not arise, but they are intrinsic to and bound up in the notion of life.

The fact of consciousness.

Consciousness (as opposed to thought) serves no function, in any purely materialistic anthropology: every aspect of what it is to be human which is identifiable as of survival value and purposive – indeed as valuable in any way – can be described and explained without ever referring to consciousness. Consciousness seems to be the one aspect of human reality which is transcendent. Consciousness is like "God" in that it too is "no thing" and "does not exist". Consciousness is the *psychological basis of value* and worth, and so of ethics and the imperative that underpins justice.

The human intuition of beauty.

Humans have an idea of beauty, and aspire to this ideal. Humans want to be beautiful themselves. Humans desire to possess and to be otherwise associated with beautiful things. The idea of absolute beauty may be delusional – but it might not be so. Humans find the notion of absolute beauty profoundly attractive. This is a fact which must not simply be discounted. It must either be accepted as evidential of some real object, or else carefully and thoroughly "explained away" as spurious in some way. It is not sufficient to dismiss the idea of "absolute beauty" out of hand as fake.

The human intuition of justice.

Humans have an idea of justice, and aspire to this ideal. Humans want to be just themselves and to live in a just society. Nowadays this manifests itself in the idea of "inalienable human rights." The idea of absolute justice may be delusional – but it might not be so. Humans find the notion of absolute justice profoundly attractive. This is a fact which must not simply be discounted. It must either be accepted as evidential of some real object, or else carefully and thoroughly "explained away" as spurious in some way. It is not sufficient to dismiss the idea of "absolute justice" out of hand as fake. Apart from anything else, if one believes that absolute justice is a spurious concept, one has no solid argument against tyranny and wickedness of any kind at all: might is then right.

God is the Greatest Conceivable Being.

The Ontological Argument for the reality of God establishes that God is the Greatest Conceivable Being. This means that every perfectible characteristic must be exemplified within the divine nature.

If justice is understood as "that state of affairs in which every constituent is fully realised and expressed in harmony and peace, without any conflict or compromise," then it is immediately clear that justice is the foundational principle of divinity: because this account of justice is exactly the basis necessary for every "perfectible characteristic" – the "constituents" of the divine nature – to cohere together as a single coherent whole.

Similarly, if beauty is understood as "that state in which order and coherence is found in a richness of diversity and on a multitude of levels," then it is recognisable as a concomitant of justice and an indication of at least its approximate presence.

This conclusion about the divine nature suggests that not only "God-as-being-God" (the "divine essence") is just, but also that "God-as-doing-what-God-does" (the "divine energies") is just: in the sense that God could not tolerate any destiny for the Cosmos (or at least its ethically significant aspects: certainly all conscious beings and perhaps all living beings) other than fulfilment and realisation, because any other outcome would conflict fundamentally with God's own nature.

The question at the head of this chapter is readily answered: "A human being is not in any relevant way like God, and so the two situations are entirely different (even assuming that the second is in any way possible) and not just different in detail."

However, this question is not really a question at all. In reality, it is the rhetorical assertion that there is no significant difference between the two cases; but this is based on the idea that God is a quasi-all-powerful being which can be put into the same category as a human being, if only remotely.

This is wrong: God is utterly incapable of any inconsistency of essence or energy (being or doing: nature or action) and so could not on the one hand bring into existence an ethically significant agent and then frustrate or oppose its innate rights, or disrespect its intrinsic dignity. In as far as it may seem that God does act in such an incoherent (and cruel) manner, this must be because we are not aware of the full picture, and/or are failing to properly understand the facts which are known to us.

The real issue here is not why one should believe that God is benevolent, it seems to me that this idea is not difficult to justify; but how one can account for injustice and suffering – especially what is called "natural evil": which is not in any way attributable to human folly or wickedness. My partial and provisional answer to this question is given in chapters 10, 11 and 12 of my book "The Good of Being".

The Problem of Suffering

The sheer amount of injustice and suffering in the world – especially what is called "natural evil" – makes it very difficult to believe in the reality of a benevolent, omnipotent God.

The "Problem of Suffering" is, I believe, the biggest problem that any serious Theist has to face. I have covered this in great depth in my book "The Good of Being" and do not intend to re-hash the arguments I present in that text here. Suffice to say that if God is benevolent and omnipotent, it follows remorselessly that the suffering experienced by conscious beings in this world must be necessary in some way. The obvious account of how this could be the case is the hypothesis that for God to protect sapient beings from all suffering would somehow undermine the entire rationale of Creation. This makes sense if the point of Creation is the moral education of sapient beings, as is strongly indicated in the Bible.

A little thought will show that for God to entirely mitigate the harmful effects which necessarily follow from the laws of Physics[1] would, first: remove what is called "moral hazard", so making "good" and "evil" equivalent[2] and, second: disincentivize sentient beings from learning about how the world works, and coming to understand both Physics and Ethics.[3]

I accept that no intellectual argument seeking to show that the suffering of conscious beings is somehow justified or necessary will ever feel right. This is because suffering is, I do not doubt, a bad thing and both the quantity and severity of suffering in our world is horrendous. Any attempt to "exonerate God" from responsibility (at least passive or negligent) for the suffering of conscious beings will never seem convincing.

---

1 Earthquakes, volcanic eruptions, hurricanes, tsunami, meteorite impacts, the effect of falling from a great height, being shot with a bullet or arrow, or of being exposed to extreme heat or cold…

2 "Good" is whatever facilitates and promotes life, whereas "evil" is whatever compromises, undermines or destroys life.

3 See pages 151–154. See also GOB cap 11.

It will always seem much more plausible that God could preclude, alleviate or mitigate any particular example of suffering, and that God's failure to do so is indicative either of God's impotence, or else of God's indifference. Only were we to see the situation clearly from God's point of view would such an argument have force;[4] and even then it would have a force which would undoubtedly produce great sorrow in addition to the unflinching resolve to step back and allow conscious beings to suffer.

The Catholic can add, of course, that God took responsibility for being complicit in the suffering of humanity by sharing in that suffering in the person of Jesus of Nazareth. In His life and passion He accepted rejection, dishonour, hatred, condemnation, torture and execution. Even now, Jesus' glorified body bears the wounds which testify to His acceptance of our condemnation of Him.[5] Even now, His Sacred Heart bleeds with sorrowful love for sinners; and with empathy for the sufferings of the poor, the lonely, the depressed, the sick, the infirm, the maimed, the addicted, the handicapped, the aged, and the dying. God in Christ Jesus' humanity knows all the sufferings of the human race – the anguish of every broken heart and ravaged body – and suffers alongside every individual in distress.

---

4   "If we could see all, all might seem good."
      [E. Thomas "As the Team's Head Brass" (1916)]
5   Thanks to A. Siddiqui for this insight.

Necessary Evil[6]

Our business is to learn that death
      is sin's most necessary recompense;
and so to choose what's right, not wrong,
      without a hint of diffidence.
This we can only do if every choice has its sure consequence.

There must be moral hazard, founded on unswerving law;
or else between wisdom and folly
      there would be no difference,
there would be no divide
      between what's reckless and prudence.

If on jumping from a precipice I did not fall to stony floor,
always being rescued by an angel's hand;[7]
      presumption hyperbolic
(that's filled with risk and self-despond)
      would be remade as merry frolic!
which would, after not long,
      become most tedious, and nothing more.

---

6   First published in "A Sparrow Falls" [S.C. Lovatt (2014)]
7   "He shall give his angels charge concerning thee: and in their hands
     they shall bear thee up, lest at any time thou dash thy foot against
     a stone." [Mat 4:6. KJV, quoting Ps 90:11-13]

The Woman's Song[5]

I don't regret I chewed that fruit;
though – for a while – it cost me life,
and gave me pain and forced my toil.
I cannot now foreswear that bite.
From swallowed seed has sprung salvation:
an end which was beyond my nature,
before I took the outlawed food:
a cause of great elation!

The serpent did not false seduce
in telling me that I would know
the good from bad if I did take and eat
its fleshy pulp and suck its ruddy juice.
This knowledge is a gift beyond all bill;
for now I am become divine[8]
and so can be God's friend,
not just some agent of His will.

For a pace, I must know strife;
so that I can in freedom learn and grow,
and come to realise what God has done
in shocking my poor soul to life;
and at the last I will be born again:
of the New Man the Mother be,
and co-redeemer of my race.
All flesh will hail me Heavenly Queen!

---

8   2Pet 1:4.

Adam's lesson[5]

If I were pre-programmed,
with Heaven I'd close agree
and I would understand
why right was right; but see
I'd then be just of God a copy.

Now I can't be of God an Isomorph:
if I were true entire, we'd be the same;
but being identical and being distinct
is quite absurd: of contradict'ry fame!
God can not shine in one corner and I in mine
like two twin magic beans in a shared pod;
for God is ev'rywhere, in all things fine;
and so would I be, if I too were God.

So I can be at best to God a Homomorph;
but I know this is just not good enough:
no shadow of what's right is just itself!
Can I become divine[7] and my own name preserve?
God's knowledge is formal and intuitive;
while ours is based on case, and hence deductive.

We can learn what God knows entirely
if it is gleaned by a diverse modality;
for then we'll know not only what it is we know,
but how we came to understand, also:
out of experience and conjecture,
which differs much from divine rapture.

Difference of personal identity
requires process and history.
So now we clearly see
the great importance of autonomy:
that I can only learn to myself be!

Job's complaint[5]

The voice of Job cries out to Heaven:
         "What have I done?
There's no just cause for all my liability
to suffer earthquake, hurricane and techtonic eruption.
Why must my best laid plans all end up in futility?
I'm plagued and starved and threatened by corruption
and after my set time by prospect of senility!"

The voice of God replies to Job:
         "Mark well these words, my son,
you've no just case against me.
For you have no idea what I've already done
for all my folk who live beneath the rainbow gay
which is my favour's pledge to all humanity.

Your notion of what by physic's law must come
is based on what you see from day to day
but this is full of my preventive action
how will you then renormalise[9] my grace away?
If I were reticent in giving benediction
the state of things would be much more awry!"

---

9   A theoretical physics term. If a thing (such as an electron) always
    appears along with a retinue; then how can one distinguish between
    the thing-in-itself and the thing-as-it-always-appears? We can only
    ever have experience of the thing-as-it-always-appears, after all!
    Sometimes it does prove possible to make this distinction: in which
    case one has achieved "re-normalisation".

Now Job retorts, in flaming woe:
        "It would be hard to bear
if only sinners came to such calamity,
but often it's the just and kind who suffer
this seems to me a great profanity!
You exploit the innocent for sport.
Not content with their servility,
You love to see their red blood spurt.
Delighting in their vulnerability
you shoot your barbs, and cut their sad lives short!"

God makes response, with kindly sense:
        "But pain and death are not as bad
as they may seem; for there's a life beyond the grave.[10]
I take no pleasure in what makes you sad
it is my will to prosper you and save
you from all ill. I have no need
for entertainment of that kind
or any other! I want you to succeed
and in this wondrous world to find
much joy! My business is for you to learn
to tell what's good from what is not,
and my unfeigned respect to earn.
Moral hazard's necessary if your sort
is ever to exceed what's natural
and so be worthy of the Life Eternal."

---

10 The fact that suffering might be recompensed post mortem does
   not justify suffering. Suffering can only be justified if it is strictly
   necessary for the achievement of some sufficiently valuable and
   desirable benefit.

But Job is not remotely satisfied, and shouts:
          "You say that we
must learn to tell what's right from wrong
by finding out the upshot of our agency;
but the actions of which my feeble tongue
makes its sincere complaint are Thine,
O God inscrutable – not mine!

What am I supposed to learn from them?
It seems, at best, that You don't care;
for if You did, You'd intervene
to stop them taking effect where
the innocent would elsewise suffer –
if You were at all just and fair."

God answers Job, most patiently:
          "An option's risk being understood,
if you take it, then that's your doom![11]
Choose active fault line as your neighbourhood,
or else the shadow of volcanic cone,
or plateau scoured often by tornadoes,
or shore which tzunamis frequent;
than you must accept all of those
outcomes which flow – or else repent.

The evils of which you make moan
are not my acts intentional
but certain and most sure outcome
of Cosmic rule conventional
which solid holds the World as One.

_____

11 Chosen path, not "extrinsic punishment".

I must not subsidise your folly
for then you could not learn.
The preservation of your autonomy
(which is a great and glorious good)
requires that I am resolute and stern.
This of my business is foundational
though repent of it I now would;
were making Man divine[7] not my whole goal."

A final point, Job pleads with God:
          "You should at least the ignorant show pity
averting dangers of which they don't know.
If they are unaware that their fair city
sits on a crack that's fit to make it rock and roll,
or have no clue their scenic mount
is filled with magma, and so soon
with pumice and with flame will fount
and like a lanced carbuncle spume;
then You should reign back every law:
for they're secure only as far
as You allow. You're able to act for
the innocent, if of them You have a care –
as You claimed when challenged by your friend,[12]
after Your first supper,[13] before the fire
on Sodom and Gomorrah did descend.
Then the innocent You saw
and You did a good while forebear!"

---

12 Abraham is one of the very few Bible characters described as being
   a friend of God. [2Chr 20:7. Is 41:8. Jas 2:23]
13 The Theophany of Mamre, when Abraham shared food with
   "The Three Angels". [Gen 18:1-8]

God then replies from the gyre of His grace:
    "If the volcano's blast ne'er hurt
those who knew not its power to harm,
and I always shielded the ignorant,
this would disincentivize the nave to learn.
Ish and Ishshah[14] were secured in Eden
by My strict pedagoguey of their innocence;
but to explore beyond that narrow glen
they had to taste experience.

If things were not how they are now,
you'd have no reason truth to know.
The more that you came to see how
things work, and did in wisdom grow;
grasping the designs of the world:
the less you would be able to rely
on my sure aid, as being curled
up in my gentle arms, safely.[15]

No sooner than you realised this fact
you'd seek out that knowledge no more
which your first paradisial state had lacked;
but rather your naïvety you would try to restore!
This would undo human autonomy
and worthy self-respect
and it's an outcome which I hope you'll see
I rightly do reject."

---

14 In chapter two of Genesis, the first humans are designated Ish
   and Ishshah before they eat the fruit of the Tree of Knowledge of
   Good and Evil. These names later take on the meaning "man"
   or "husband" and "woman" or "wife".

15 It was a "necessary fault" that Adam should "sin" (be separated
   from God) if Adam was ever to ascend to a state of quasi-equality
   of God by the process of "divinization". [2Pet 1:4.]

Religion is fake

Looking at many cultures, religion seems to be a fabricated response to life's problems.

Religion in general is indeed "a response to life's problems". In as far as it is a human response it is fabricated, but this doesn't mean that it is wrong or bad. Science, engineering and Art are all human fabrications – and valuable just the same. The fact that I don't think that Plato's writings are divinely inspired (and that many of the stories he tells of Socrates are fabricated) does not mean that they are invalid, or of doubtful value.

Moreover the fact that a thing might be fabricated in the very worst sense doesn't mean that it is wrong. Even if the story of the Exodus and of the Twelve Tribes of Israel was fabricated by a small group of Levites in order to serve as a myth which would form the basis of a national identity for a coalition of Caananite tribes which they were trying to cement together into a single society, this fictional story would have a validity quite apart from its historical falsity.

It would be what Plato calls "a royal lie"[1] and set forth a truth (that it is not necessary to be blood relatives in order to have common cause in a State) in a way that was acceptable to the mentality of the time. Later on in the Bible there is a clear statement of this where it is said that the Gentiles will be called to Jerusalem[2] and when they arrive each will have their name entered into a census roll, as having been born there.[3] This is the blatant fabrication of a historically false record; but the purpose is righteous, admirable, and just.

---

1   Plato "Republic" 2:382c-d; 3:389b-c, 414b-415d.
2   Is 66:18-23.
3   Ps 86.

Lack of alternative is no proof

The fact that there doesn't seem to be any better way to give life value doesn't make religion any more convincing.

If it were true that life has value, and that it was clear that there was no way to account for this fact apart from adopting a "religious" view of reality, then this would in fact be a solid proof of the truth of "religion". It is easier for a mathematician or logician to see this than anyone uneducated in these disciplines. Very often in Mathematics or Logic one proves some proposition or formula by disproving its opposite: by showing that the opposite unavoidably results in some absurd conclusion. Hence it an entirely adequate justification for "religious faith" would be the two statements:

1. It is certain that there is no solid basis for value or ethics, apart from religious faith,
2. It is absolutely required that value and/or ethics has a solid basis.

However, the second statement is not obviously true. After all many people deny it in their words, even if they act as if it is true. Nevertheless, it seems to me that any deviation from it inevitably results in a spiral into moral Relativism and even Nihilism. Moreover, it is difficult to see how one could show exhaustively that adopting "religion" was the *only* way to underpin life as a basis for value. Nevertheless, a conviction that life has value coupled with the fact that "there doesn't seem to be any better way to give life value" is a compelling, if not conclusive, argument in favour of "religion".

Technically, I don't think that "life has value." Rather, I think that life is what gives value to other things, while not being valuable itself. Just as God is the "uncaused first cause",

so "life is the invaluable source of value."[1] Moreover,
it isn't religion or religious faith which underpins life as the
source of value, but "the eternal dimension to human existence":
the idea that, somehow, our actions and experiences have
a permanence, persistence, robustness, solidity and significance
to them which cannot be accounted for in terms of materialism.[2]

On a Catholic account of things, Ethics and the basis of value
are not matters of revelation: rather, they are issues which are
amenable to the unaided light of human reason, and so accessible
to any person of good-will irrespective of their having any
religious faith – and definitely independent of whether or not they
are Catholic.

The Catholic religion is very much concerned with these
issues, of course; but not as making a claim to be itself the
foundation or source of Ethics – either in specifics or generality.
It is part of the proper business of the Church's hierarchy
to clarify and bring into sharp focus what we can come to know
for ourselves; to corroborate and confirm us in those conclusions
which we ought to be able to attain on our own autonomous
account; to encourage us when what we know is right seems
too difficult for us to practice; to admonish us when we fall short
of righteousness; and to applaud us when we manage to live up to
the demands of justice.

---

1   GOB caps 4&5.
2   UPSY. GOB cap 5 & 9.

The problem of particularity

The specificity of religion makes it seem like a lottery. Accident of birth and/or experience seems to play much too much a role in whether a person even has the chance to consider – let alone accept – the teachings and practices of any particular faith.

I call this "The Problem of Particularity".[1] In brief, I reply that what really matters is not whether a person has religious faith, or belongs to a particular group, but whether they "hunger and thirst for righteousness."[2] Jesus' "Parable of the Talents"[3] makes it clear that what matters is what we make of what we are given:

> From everyone to whom much has been given, much will be required; and from the one to whom much has been entrusted, even more will be demanded.
> [Lk 12:48. NRSV]

Hence the fewer opportunities a person has to make spiritual progress, the more significant is the spiritual progress which they do make: even if this seems small, or even negligible, to an outside observer. The writer of Hebrews tells us that

> Whoever would draw near to God must believe that He exists and that He rewards those who seek Him.
> [Heb 11:6 RSV]

which makes no mention of adherence to any specific creed. Moreover, the Apostle Paul writes

> When Gentiles who have not the law do by nature what the law requires, they are a law to themselves, even though they do not have the law. [Rom 2:14 RSV]

---

1 GOB cap 17.
2 Mat 5:6. RSV
3 Mat 25:14-28.

Elsewhere he makes it clear that:

> the living God, which made heaven, and earth, and the
> sea, and all things that are therein, Who in times past
> suffered all nations to walk in their own ways... **left not
> Himself without witness,** in that He did good, and gave
> us rain from heaven, and fruitful seasons, filling our
> hearts with food and gladness. [Acts 14:17 RSV]

Explicit, visible membership of the Church is not itself a prize
to be obtained, or a necessary condition for pleasing God;
but a help and assistance to an end: salvation. The sacraments
and the Gospel Revelation are not primarily challenges, still less
obstacles; but more accurately *means to cheat the system*:
crib notes we are allowed to take into the exam, and steroids
we are allowed to inject before the race, if you like.
They are provided not so much for our personal betterment
(though they do serve this purpose, of course) but so as to allow
us as individuals to achieve together as a community more than
we could ever do on our own, alone. They are provided to enable
us to start constructing a ramshackle preview of The Kingdom
of God, so that we can begin to practice the lifestyle we will have
to pursue and sustain once God has renovated Heaven and Earth,
and the dead are raised again from their graves to eternal life.
This ramshackle preview is then itself meant to be a testimony
to non-believers of what is possible and to serve as an invitation
to them to get involved with God's salvation project.

*Are you then implying that many people do not need
to be Catholic, even if they have the opportunity?
Catholicism is supposed to be universal is it not?*

The Church indeed is Catholic, and this means both that
everyone is welcome to join and that all have a duty to join.
However, the only thing that anyone **needs** to be is "just".
The Church teaches that it is impossible for anyone to be made
just except with God's help. The Church further teaches that
everyone who is being made just is a member of the Church

in some way or other. It is very much better for everyone concerned if this membership is explicit and acknowledged, but it does not absolutely have to be so.

Anyone who has a real opportunity to visibly join the Church and refuses to do so (or who is a member and then apostatises) thereby commits a mortal sin; but what looks like a real opportunity may not in fact be such. This is the point of the idea of *invincible ignorance*, by which is meant some psychological or social impediment which makes it morally impossible for an individual either to recognise the Church for what it is, or else to realise that they have an obligation to join the Church. As to how many people are *hidden or anonymous Catholics*, and how many are impeded from joining the Church by their *invincible ignorance*, I cannot say. One can hope that most Protestants are *invincibly ignorant*, but as for the run of the mill unchurched, I have no idea.

Equivalently, if a Catholic apostatises because they have been scandalised by the offensive teaching or example of clergy or senior laity, I would lay the blame for this in the lap of those who *broke the bruised reed and quenched the smoking flax*,[4] rather than the apostate themselves. It is entirely possible that the material apostate acted in accordance with their conscience in giving up on the Church, and it may have been their solemn duty before God to do so: the only way for them to maintain their connexion with God.

I know of one person who gave up on the Catholic Church because he decided that if he continued to practice as a Catholic it would be so psychologically harmful to him that it would in all likelihood send him mad and destroy his faith in God. He had experienced very bad pastoral *care* in confession, and seen Sunday Mass celebrated in such an irreverent manner that he simply could not bear it.

As far as anyone is concerned, the only facts that matters are that they are themselves welcome to join the Church, and have an obligation to do so. How God may or may not deal with other people is not their concern, beyond the facts that God "desires that

---

4   Is 42:3. Mt 12:20.

all men be saved and come to the knowledge of the truth",[5] that "everyone receives sufficient grace to be saved"[6] and "God's grace extends beyond the visible and organisational Church and is not limited to the Sacraments."[7]

Particularity Sylogism

P1   God is just.
P1.1   God ought to treat all sapient beings equitably.
P1.2   God ought to treat all sapient beings equivalently.
P1.3   God ought to treat all sapient beings identically.

P2   All religions are localised in space and time.
P2.1   They have a beginning with either a single person, or else in a small community; at either a particular time, or else as a result of some particular gradual historic process.
P2.2   They have a geographical region in which they are concentrated: generally as a result of how they originated.
P2.3   Hence, every religion is inaccessible to a wide range of people: those who died before it came into being; those who never got to hear about it, because the message did not reach their neighbourhood before they died; and those who had their minds poisoned against the religion by false representations made of it by its opponents.

P3   Hence, every religion is, of necessity, contrary to "P1.3".
P3.1   Hence, no religion can be important; for if it were important this would infringe "P1.3".
P3.2   It seems more plausible to assert that every religion is, of necessity, unjust because of its character of "particularity" ["P2.1–2.3"] which infringes "P1.3".
P3.3   It seems more plausible to assert that all that matters is that a human being "tries to live a good life" and as far as any eternal destiny is concerned, just "hopes for the best."

---

5   Jn 1:7; 12:32. 1Cor 10:33. 1Tim 2:4.
6   FCD lib 4.1 sec 1 cap 3 #11.
7   See page 168ff.

Reply

R1 Justice does not imply "equality of treatment"! Different sapient beings are different in nature and so require different treatment if one is to do justice towards and by them. Hence "P1.3" is formally false. However, "P1.3" still has some force; because it does not seem that the differences among human beings are either sufficient in magnitude, or of appropriate character, to justify the difference in treatment which the particularity of religion would seem to require if it were to be compatible with justice.

R1.1 Justice seems to requires that every sapient conscious being has the appropriate opportunity to be "saved". This is standard Catholic doctrine.[6]

R1.2 Arguably, justice requires that every sapient conscious being is "saved"; but this presumes that "saved" is a good category. The Bible makes it clear that it is God's definite will that every human being is "saved" and yet strongly suggests that, in spite of this, not all human beings are "saved".

R1.3 It is better to state that justice requires that every sapient conscious being attains whatever end, destiny, fulfilment is appropriate for it.

R1.4 This invites the question: "What is the appropriate fulfilment for each sapient conscious being, and might this differ hugely in character?" If so, it might be the case that – in divine providence – each human being is born into exactly that situation and context which is appropriate for them; but I find this proposition most unsatisfying and unconvincing!

R1.5 The particularity of Judaism is partly justified by the idea that it is not necessary to be a Jew to "be saved" and that Gentiles can be saved too – and may even find it easier to achieve salvation than Jews do. However, the fact that not all Gentiles have had the opportunity of benefiting from the moral example of good Jews still attracts the criticism of "P3.1".

R1.6 Those religions which envisage reincarnation can escape the syllogism presented here. They can assert that karma determines whether a soul has the decided advantage of being a part of the religion in question. So, for example: every soul which has good karma will be given the opportunity to be a Buddhist, and every soul with bad karma will be denied that opportunity. They will get another opportunity as soon as they have "worked off" their bad karma.

R1.7 Those religions (eg Calvinism and some varieties of Islam) which discount human free-will can escape the syllogism presented here. They can assert that God creates certain souls with the specific destiny of being damned: they are crafted purposefully in such a manner that this is their appropriate fulfilment. The problem with this position is that it invites the question: "Why would God create conscious sapient beings of such a character?" This seems to be unanswerable, and in any case is contrary to the explicit teaching of the Bible!

R1.8 Those religions (e.g. Confucianism, Shinto and, perhaps, Daoism) which make no claims about "salvation" but only about "successful living" (or similar) conform to "P3.1".

R1.9 The "Problem of Particularity" only really applies to Monotheistic "salvation" religions, namely: Judaism, Christianity, Islam – and their derivatives, such as Mormonism.

R2 On the assumption that "saved" is a good category and that "free-will" has some kind of validity, "P1" implies that "Every human being must have an adequate opportunity to be saved."

R2.1 If the idea of free-will is misleading, then the concept of opportunity is liable to be empty of meaning and one seems to be forced back to the idea that every sapient conscious being is "saved": "Universalism" – as proposed by Origen of Alexandria and his followers.[8]

---

8   FCD lib 5 cap 1.4 #3a

R3 It is a basic belief of Catholicism that every human soul has access to the Natural Law and so has the ability – quite apart from God's help – of knowing what is right and what is wrong and how to live a righteous life. This is stated explicitly in the Bible by both St Paul and St John.[9]

R3.1 It is a defined dogma of Catholicism that it is possible to come to a knowledge of God's reality by the unaided light of human reason, from the fact and character of physical existence.[10] This is stated explicitly in the Bible.[11]

R3.2 The writer of the epistle to the Hebrews states that "whoever would draw near to God must believe that He exists and that He rewards those who seek him,"[12]

R3.3 Jesus states that "Blessed are those who hunger and thirst for righteousness: for they shall be satisfied."[13]

R3.4 Jesus states that those who care for the needy will be saved, whether or not they acknowledge Him explicitly as Lord.[14]

R3.5 It is a leading idea of Catholic thought that "every soul receives sufficient grace to be saved."[6] This includes those who have not been baptised, and also all those who are excluded from hearing the Gospel by the particularity of Catholicism.

R3.6 Catholicism rejoices in the "salvation" of many Old Testament characters: Adam and Eve, Enoch, Abraham, Israel, Moses, Samuel, David, Elijah and so on. The "holy innocents" who were killed by King Herod when he was trying to assassinate Jesus are also presented as "being saved" though they knew nothing of Christ.

R3.7 Taking "R3.1 – R3.6" seriously would seem to admit "P3.1" and undermine Catholicism's claim to be of great importance.

---

9   Rom 2:14. Jn 1:4, 9.
10 FCD lib 1 part 1 sec 1 cap 1 §1 #1
11 Wis 13:5. Rom 1:19-20.
12 Heb 11:6. RSV
13 Mat 5:6. RSV
14 Mat 25:34-40.

R4 It would seem that the most that Catholicism can claim – but this is a great deal! – is that it has a clearer view of the character of God, and of God's business with Creation – and in particular with human beings – than any other religion; and that it has "means of grace" (that is, the sacraments) which are of an entirely different order of reality than anything on offer from any other religion.

R4.1 Catholicism does not claim that it is necessary to be a "paid-up" Catholic in order to be saved; but only that it makes it a great deal easier to live a life which is directed towards salvation.

R4.2 This is easier in the sense that there is more help on offer; hence either a successful outcome is more to be expected, or else the path to a successful outcome will be more pleasant – on the basis that it is much better to know why a dentist or surgeon is doing painful things to one than simply to experience the pain while having no notion that the person inflicting it has both a benevolent intention and the expertise necessary to govern their well-intentioned action.

R4.3 An additional claim which Catholicism can make is that it is God's means of laying the foundations within time of the "Kingdom of God" which will arise from the Church "at the end of the Ages". This foundation requires a population of people to do the excavation and laying of stones; however they do this not just for their own benefit, but rather for the benefit of everyone who is saved. This ties in with the partial justification of Jewish Particularity, and completes it: for if this proposition regarding the Catholic Church is true, then it validates the Jewish salvation-history also, as being the bed-rock upon which the Catholic Church is itself founded.

Salvation: individual and corporate[15]

The Church does not simply exist to facilitate the salvation of individuals, through baptism, instruction, enlightenment and justification. Individuals also exist to facilitate the salvation of society, through the establishment of the Kingdom of God. Each of us is appointed in this mortal life with certain responsibilities. For some, these are primarily the care and ruling of their own souls, which is the contemplative vocation; for others, they are the care and ruling of others, which is the active or apostolic vocation.

> It is better for everyone to be ruled by divine reason, preferably within himself and his own, otherwise imposed from without, so that as far as possible all will be alike and friends, governed by the same thing.
> [Plato "Republic" (9:590d)]

We have, first, the commission to use the talents which God has given us and, second, the daily opportunities to do so – for our own good and the good of our neighbour. As we respond either well or badly to the vocation we have been given, we either help the cause of justice (both interiorly, in our own soul, and exteriorly in society at large) or else harm it. If we learn from the process, we become fit for Eternal Life; if we do not, then we remain unfit for life in God's Kingdom.

Salvation history is the process by which human society is gradually being transformed from injustice into justice – from the Kingdom of Man into the Kingdom of God – just as each individual life is the opportunity for a soul to be uplifted from depravity into holiness.

> The kingdom of heaven is like leaven which a woman took and hid in three measures of flour, till it was all leavened. [Mat 13:33 RSV]

---

15 GOB cap 17.

None of God's interventions in human affairs should be understood as favouring those persons who directly receive God's message, commission or help. Always, one should interpret God's particular interventions as being for the general good. Any grace received by an individual or group is granted for the service of those not directly involved, and always comes with a responsibility towards those who are not immediately affected. Just as the Jews were chosen by God not for their own advantage but for the good of the Gentiles,[16] so the Catholic Church does not exist primarily for the benefit of its members; but rather for the salvation of non-Catholics; and not so much by their conversion to Catholicism as by the ethical effect on their consciences of the example that Catholics should be setting in their daily lives.

> We are not called to discipleship to be saved, but are called to discipleship in order to announce salvation to others. Those who are saved are those who do the Father's will; whether or not they are professed disciples.[17] On the other hand, even if a disciple has been a disciple for long and has prayed time and again in the way that they ought, they will not enter the Kingdom of God if they fail to do God's will.[18]
>
> The Good News, therefore, is that those who fulfil the beatitudes,[19] whether or not they are professed disciples, will enter the kingdom of heaven. And the purpose of being a disciple of Christ is to make this Gospel known to all nations, and so to make disciple to continue the mission. Now, if that was the whole of the Gospel, it would be rather depressing for sinners; but in fact there is also the part about God saving sinners. This should not be understood to conflict with the commission to tell the poor in spirit, those who mourn, the meek, those who

16 Gen 12:3. Ps 66; 95; 116. Is 42:1-6; 49:3-7; 66:16-23. Jer 1:5; 3:17. Micah 4:1-3. Zech 2:10-11; 8:18-23. Jonah. Sir 44:19-23.
17 Lk 9:40-50. Rom 2:6-16.
18 Mat 7:21.
19 Mat 5:1-12.

hunger and thirst for righteousness, the merciful, the pure of heart, the peacemakers and those persecuted for the sake of the cause of justice, that their hope is not in vain: whether or not they are professed disciples.

Notice how another part of the disciples' mission is to have faith and to propagate faith. This is made particularly obvious when the disciples fail to heal as requested and expected to do.[20] The reason, they are told, is because of a lack of faith, and this lack of faith is what enrages Christ. The point, I think, is not that you need to believe in order to work miracles (for Christ almost never says that it is His faith that has healed the sick) but the faith of the afflicted person or their sponsor that has healed them. In other words, it is not one's own faith in God that works the miracles, rather it is the spreading of faith to others (by a disciplined life of prayer and fasting[21]) that people can be healed and that the Kingdom of God is at hand.[22]

The purpose of discipleship and of the disciples' commission, is not only to encourage long-suffering righteous folk, nor merely to go announce the good news of redemption to sinners and sick, but to spread an attitude or perspective of faith. This insistence on spreading faith defines the sort of love which disciples are also mandated to spread. It is not a dispassionate humanitarianism that they are told to promote, but a love filled with eschatalogical hope; since it is that sort of hope which makes faith – and so miracles possible.

[J.F. Garneau "Private Communication" (2012)]

---

20 Mat 17:14-20. Mk 9:14-29.
21 Mk 9:29 RSV, Catholic edition.
22 Mat 3:2; 4:17; 19:7. Mk 1:15.

Plato's Republic

Plato had a vision of a Kingdom of Justice. He describes it in more prescriptive terms than does Jesus, and some of his ideas (especially the systematic destruction of family life) strike the modern ear as ludicrous and even inhumane. Nevertheless, Plato's motives were close to those of Jesus. Both of them were concerned to establish a society of mutual care based on friendship and equity; where all was ordered, harmonious and peaceful, and where there was no conflict, pain or suffering. When faced with the impossibility of ever establishing such a society Plato opined that:

> No city, constitution, or individual man will ever become perfect until either some chance event compels those few philosophers who aren't vicious... to take charge of a city... and compels the city to obey them, or until a god inspires the present rulers and kings or their offspring with a true erotic love for true Philosophy... Then the philosopher, by consorting with what is ordered and divine and despite all the slanders around that say otherwise, himself becomes as divine and ordered as a human being can... One such individual would be sufficient to bring to completion all the things that now seem so incredible, providing that his city obeys him. [Plato "Republic" (6:499b-502b)]

This can be taken as a prophecy of Jesus, who was the offspring of King David and who had "a true erotic love for true Philosophy"[23] and who was "as divine and ordered as is humanly possible" and who founded the Church as a seed[24] which has the potential to grow into the completion of all things,[25] providing only that the potential citizens of His heavenly city obey Him.

---

23 Mat 7:24; 10:16; 24:45; 25:1-9. Lk 12:42. Jn 8:23-47; 18:37-38.
24 Jn 12:24; 31-33.
25 Mat 13:31-32. Mk 4:31. Lk 13:19. Eph 1:15-23.

Building bridges and breaking-down barriers

Every division exists to be broken down; the demolition of division being the prime business of the Church, following on from the initiative of Christ.[26] Hence, the rich exist to serve the poor and find their salvation in fulfilling this role.[27] The poor and infirm exist so that those more fortunate might care for them and alleviate their distress. They obtain a presentiment of divine love in the care which they receive. Similarly, the ignorant exist so that the wise might school them and the wise exist to do so. Both wise and ignorant benefit from this educative process, learning from each other's questions and answers.

The business of the Church is to become the true Tower of Babel. The original Babel project was inspired by hubris and conceit. God's New Babel project is a very different affair. The Church gathers together people of all races, giving them a single voice, uniting them in the common task of establishing friendship across all nations, and directing them in the construction of God's Eternal City;[28] which will tower over its foundations into the Heavens. Not everyone is called to contribute directly (still less equally) in the construction of this city; but all are expected to strive to become its worthy citizens.[29] All are welcome to enter its courts and to find refuge, solace and joy there. All are invited to dwell in this divine metropolis.

---

26 Eph 2:10-22. Gal 3:23-29.

27 Mat 25:31-40.

28 Heb 11:16; 12:22.

29 1Cor 9:24-25. 1Tim 4:7-10. In "Republic" Plato teaches that social justice and interior justice mirror each other, so the two vocations are not clearly distinct. Similarly, the Apostle Peter tells us that we are each living stones to be built together into God's spiritual house [1Pet 2:5] and the Apostle Paul teaches that we are each organs of the one Body of Christ. [Rom 12:4. 1Cor 12:12-27]

Religion is ineffective

Religion doesn't seem to have any significant effect on either a person's well-being, or on their character and ethic.

The first assertion contained here (that religion doesn't enhance a person's well-being) is countered by empirical evidence. There are many studies that show a high correlation between "religious practice" or "belonging to some religious community" and both physical and psychological well-being. This is not surprising – indeed it would be surprising if it were not true – and is readily explained. The issue of the truth of the religion involved doesn't come into this question at all.

Religion is, at the very least, a "fabricated response to life's problems." This means that it is intended to serve the purpose of giving comfort in distress, hope in despair, and certainty in confusion. It is pretty much inevitable that over time people searching for effective means to deal with the issues which religion is supposed to address will have stumbled across – and then developed and perfected – practices which alleviate distress, despair and confusion; hence it is to be expected that religious practice will reduce stress levels, and this alone is sufficient to justify an expectation that it will be beneficial, both psychologically and physiologically. I am sure that some kinds of religious practice trigger the release of endorphins, which would also tend to increase both feelings of well-being and also objectively enhance a person's mental and physical health.

The question of "miracles" and (sacramental) "grace" as objective and very significant supplements to the naturalistic account of the benefits of religious practice is, of course, an additional – and more difficult – question. Once it is admitted that religious practices like "prayer", "meditation", "communal singing", "dancing" and "participating in rituals" are liable to have positive effects irrespective of the truth of any religion's dogmatic framework, it will be difficult to disentangle these "placebo" effects from any effects attributable to "divine grace".

The second assertion (that religion doesn't improve a person's character or ethic) is impossible to establish. It is clear to me that my faith serves to underpin my ethic, and that if I did not believe in God I would have no reason to abide by any norms of behaviour apart from the fear of being "found out", and various irrational inhibitions and personal likes and dislikes. It is also clear to me that many people who practice religion – even Catholicism – do not allow the core tenets of the faith they profess to season their lifestyle or behaviour. People talk about mercy, compassion, and empathy while acting unjustly, and on the basis of irrational prejudice, without consideration or respect for others, and sometimes in a vengeful manner. This is very sad, but it is an indictment of human beings, not of religion.

There are, of course, many examples of people who are willing to testify that their lives were turned around as a result of some kind of religious conversion: drug users who were freed of their addictions; people filled with anger and hate who found peace; thieves who gave up stealing; gang-members who renounced conflict and violence; people who knew only anxiety and despair who found new meaning in their existence. These people would not agree that religion had no effect on their lifestyles, morality or outlook.

> Catholics have, to be sure, carried out countless atrocious injustices against innocent people in the name of their faith; but on balance, I believe many many more Catholics have performed acts of kindness to many many more people, inspired by hearing the Gospel, and by following the example of our saints. Please know that that is a very difficult sentence for me to write, as I think on the conduct of the Spanish Catholics encountering my brothers and sisters the Native Americans. God save me, I hope what I wrote is correct.
> [Private Communication from a friend]

Only in Catholicism (and Orthodoxy) is there the idea that there are objective means of grace which can be hoped to help one to be a better person. Other religions have various ascetic practices which it is claimed will help a person to become "better" in one way or another, if they are faithfully followed; but on such an account of things any failure to "improve" can be attributed to a failure to follow the ascetic practice properly. The Sacraments, however, are supposed to necessarily "effect what they symbolise" (as far as the disposition of the recipient allows) so it is much more of an embarrassment to Catholicism and Orthodoxy when those who regularly avail themselves of sacramental assistance (in the Eucharist and Penance) demonstrate no signs of any growth in holiness.

It would be disappointing and embarrassing for the Church if it were to be shown that the average Catholic has a worse character than the average Atheist. However this would not prove that "being a Catholic doesn't improve a person's character or ethic." It might be that the worst kind of person is drawn to Catholicism and substantially bettered by their involvement with the Church, while people who are less reprobate feel no need to associate with the Church. After all, Jesus said: "I come not to call the righteous, but sinners."[1]

If a Catholic can argue that a Buddhist or Hindu has a false religion, despite any psychological or other benefits that religion might give, then it seems that the same argument can be reversed on the Catholic.

The fact that a religious practice is beneficial does not prove the truth of the religion to which that practice is attached; however this statement has no force. It certainly does not mean that any particular religion is false. Your response has only arisen because you were originally arguing that religion was entirely ineffective. I have elsewhere stated that religious experience in general is not a good basis for faith, just as a lack of personal religious experience is not a good basis for rejecting religion.

---

1   Mt 9:13 RSV.

Religion is authoritarian

While Secularism seems to necessarily entail a spiralling into moral relativism – and even Nihilism – religion seems to involve an oppressive authoritarian dogmatism. It is unclear to me that the former is worse than the latter.

There is, undoubtedly, a tendency in *organised* religion towards "oppressive authoritarian dogmatism", and this tendency is reprehensible and damaging to individuals. However it is not religion, and still less Catholicism, which is the origin of this malady. This is indicated by two observations.

The first is that "oppressive authoritarian dogmatism" appears in a wide range of religions. This suggests that the cause of this phenomenon lies, not in any particular creedal system, but rather in some aspect of human nature, which takes whatever means lying to hand as tools of control, domination and oppression. The second is that "oppressive authoritarian dogmatism" also features strongly in the secular sphere. Political movements (such as Marxism, Socialism, Nationalism and Fascism) exhibit very similar tendencies. Moreover in my experience self-styled liberals often prove to be some of the most oppressive and authoritarian dogmatists.

Secularism does entail a spiralling into moral relativism. This is a much worse phenomenon than "oppressive authoritarian dogmatism", as it can easily encompass the latter (where a fatuous certainty is vigorously promoted so as to to fend-off the horror of the unacknowledged moral vacuum which underlies Secularism) and, unlike "oppressive authoritarian dogmatism", it cannot be critiqued, or coherently opposed, in its own terms.

In stark contrast, Christ clearly teaches with dogmatic authority that there is no place for oppressive authoritarianism within the Church, and wherever this phenomenon appears it is immediately subject to the direct condemnation of Jesus' words.[1]

> Every person carries within himself a project of God, a personal vocation, a personal idea of God... a living Temple of his presence. And the priest's role is above all to reawaken this awareness, to help the individual discover his personal vocation... Only if a living awareness of the faith illumines our hearts can we also build a just society.[2]
>
> It is not the Magisterium that imposes doctrine. It is the Magisterium that helps enable the conscience itself to hear God's voice, to know what is good, what is the Lord's will. It is only an aid so that personal responsibility, nourished by a lively conscience, may function well and thus contribute to ensuring that justice is truly present in our society: justice within ourselves and universal justice for all our brothers and sisters in the world today[2]...
>
> The Church offers us the encounter with Christ, with the living God, with the Logos who is Truth and Light, who does not coerce consciences, does not impose a partial doctrine but helps us ourselves to be men and women who are completely fulfilled and thus to live in personal responsibility and in deeper communion with one another,[2] a communion born from communion with God, with the Lord. [Benedict XVI "Greeting to the Pastoral Council of the Roman Parish of St Felicity and her children" (25th Mar 2007)]

---

1   Mk 9:35; 10:42-45. Jn 13:14.
2   Pope Benedict XVI insists on the link between – in Platonic terms – "interior or personal justice" and "exterior or societal justice."

Whom does the Christian obey? Nobody but God, and their conscience. No order or command of any sort must ever be followed by a Christian, without that Christian's complete wholehearted agreement that compliance is in accord with God's will, and with that Christian's conscience.

In Christianity, there ought to be no such thing as servile obedience, the obedience of a slave to his master. There must always be a persuasion, an instruction, to the end that the Christian understands that what is commanded is clearly in accord with the will of God, and sees also that they fully, without being forced, agrees that the end in view is a good thing, and that that includes their own good.

Unfortunately, throughout the history of the Church, hierarchs of one kind or another have stood up and commanded those under them socially, claiming they spoke In the Name of God, to perform difficult and unpleasant labours, or to submit themselves to unjust punishments. They are simply liars, and the courageous among us will call them such, and will send them away. [Private Communication, from a friend]

Atheism[3]

"I don't need to believe to be good.
I don't have to worship to know wonder.
Transcendence lies in the human heart,
not in any tabernacle, nor on any altar.
Faith and hope are empty lies,
peddled by pederasts in scarlet bold.
Love is all I need.
Love will, in the centre, hold.
Love will all my urgent hungers feed."

"A life well-lived is good enough for me.
This is the goal to which I must aspire:
the satisfactions of artistry,
and the achievements of craft,
are my deepest desire;
the explanations of science
and the consolations of philosophy
are what my mind does most require.
What more can any soul of right demand?"

"Still: what is good?" my mind uneasily inquires.
"What counts a life well-lived – and why?
All that I am, and do, and have, will pass away;
and, at the last, I know that I shall die.
So what's the end of being good?
What is the gain of courage bold?

_____

3   First published in "Building Blocks" (2014)

How can justice make its cold call
effective, and with right, in my sad soul,
if all must come to naught
but tepid death of Second Law's report?
To live for passing thrill, for fleeting ease,
is prospect not enough to my soul please;
and yet, what else is present in this futile place?"

"Why do I yearn for satisfaction
when all I know makes faith a fiction?
If hope is false, then I must own it so;
and take despair as my sole trove,
determining to never let it go:
clutching it fast to my sore breast
as treasure and object of my love
and let it suck the life from me.
If this despite is my sole progeny
then I must feed and fold and nurture it
as best I can: though there's no sense
in this that I can see."

The Bible is fictional

*Many parts of the Bible seem very "made up",
and this leads me to wonder whether the more plausible
parts are also fictitious.*

Parts of the Bible are certainly made up, in the sense of being
myth, legend, fable, parable or poetry. I doubt that the story
of Noah is remotely historical, for example, and I am pretty
sure that the stories of Jonah, Ruth and Naomi and Job are all
parabolic. As for the stories of Abraham, Isaac, Jacob-Israel,
and Joseph, I just don't know. I hope that these were real people,
and that the stories we have about them are more or less true;
but I can't be sure of this, and in any case the point of their stories
is more what we can learn from what happens than their factual
historicity. In the case of the story of King Saul, I almost hope
that this isn't historically true: his story is so tragic[1] that I'd prefer
it to be fictitious.

The fact that some books (or parts of books) in the Bible
are myth, legend, fable, parable or poetry does not in any way
imply that more plausible parts are also fictitious. It does mean
that we should be circumspect in attributing historicity to them
in a naïve manner, of course.

The two contrasting (one could say either contradictory
or complementary, depending on ones perspective or prejudice)
nativity stories found in the Gospels may well be fables;
but if this is so, that would not mean that the rest of the Gospel
accounts of Jesus' life are anything other than honest attempts
at history. It is easy to conceive that Matthew and Luke prepended
fictional birth narratives to their factual accounts of Jesus'
teaching, miracles, passion, death and resurrection because they
knew that some sort of origin story was required. We must be
wary of judging the writers of classical texts in terms of Twenty-
First Century ethics and cultural norms. What may seem improper
to us, might have seemed necessary to them.

---

1   1Sam 15.

Some Bible stories (in particular the stories of the first humans and of Noah) are much more powerful if understood as myths with no historical content at all. On that basis one is free to accept as irrelevant various awkward aspects of the plot: dismissing them as artifices required to make the story work as a means of communicating ethical or ontological truth. Moreover, one can then accept that the story does not unfold as a result of psychological or social dynamics, but rather because of the requirements of the lesson(s) to be learned by the target audience of the myth. One doesn't then ask "why did Cain slay Able?" seeking an answer in terms of Cain's psychology; rather one asks "What does it mean for Cain to slay Able?" Similarly, one is then free to ask "What does it mean for God to 'mark' Cain so that no-one would take revenge on him for his fratricidal act?"

It is possible that some Bible stories are intended to challenge us to object to what they seem to mean on a first reading. It was in this way that the rabbis came to understand the Torah injunction "to stone to death a recalcitrant son"[2] to mean that no father should ever think of his son as being recalcitrant; but instead cut him some slack as he passes through adolescence. Moreover, they came to an even deeper conclusion: that the Torah poses this advice in such an obscure way so as to teach the indefinitely more significant lesson that it is important for human beings to think through ethical issues as autonomous moral agents, rather than simply obeying injunctions as docile servants; because this is how they can gain personal ethical expertise[3] (otherwise known as wisdom or holiness) and so become "friends of God."[4]

You seem to argue that just because one part may be made up this just means we should be circumspect about which parts are historical and which are legendary, mythical or parabolic; but it seems to me that

---

2   Deut 21:19-21.
3   Sanhedrin 71a.
4   Wis 7:14, 27-28. Ps 24:14.

if an important event such as the circumstances of Jesus' birth might be fictional, then why not Calvary and the resurrection as well?

I tend to the view that central parts of both the Old Testament and New Testament are, in their key elements, historically accurate; but I can see that even if they are not historically true, they could be true in a deeper sense – and that it is this sense which is important, not the historic.

The reason historic truth is at all important in Judaism and Christianity is that both faiths are insistent on the idea that God cares about human beings, and is involved in their concerns, and is willing to get involved in their lives as a source of liberation and salvation. This fixation is pretty much unique to Judaism and the other faiths to which it has given rise: Christianity, Islam and Mormonism.

Without the examples of Abraham's intimacy with God,[5] Jacob-Israel's personal encounter with God,[6] Moses and the Exodus,[7] Joshua,[8] Samson[9] and the other Judges, the prophet Samuel[10] and King David,[11] the miracles of Elijah[12] and Elisha,[13] the return from the Babylonian Captivity[14] and the Liberation from Greek rule under the Maccabees;[15] the story of the Hebrews-Israelites-Jews hasn't any substance.

The circumstances of Jesus' birth are not very significant. True, they fulfil a few prophecies; but the reason that Christmas is deemed important is simply that the story of a baby being born,

---

5   Gen 18.
6   Gen 32:24-25.
7   Ex 32:7-14, 30-33; 33:9-11.
8   Num 27:18-22. Josh 1:5.
9   Jdg 16.
10 1Sam 3:4-20.
11 1Sam 16:13.
12 1Kgs 17-19
13 2Kgs 2:1-15; 4:1-37; 5:1-19.
14 2Chr 36:22-23. Ezr 1:1-8. Is 44:28; 45:1.
15 1Mac 4.

whatever the details, generally appeals to people on an instinctive and sentimental level. The only thing of basic dogmatic importance in Jesus' birth is that He was born to a human female, and this is not in doubt – unless He was an extraterrestrial, or some kind of Docetist phantasm.

Moreover at least three accounts can be given of the infancy narratives, not just two.

1. The Gospel accounts are, more or less, historically accurate.
2. The Gospel accounts are largely fictitious, and intended to deceive.
3. The Gospel writers were aware that they were fabricating stories, but were impelled to do so by a divinely inspired conviction that this was appropriate and indeed necessary, as serving God's providential purpose.[16] In this case, while their words were superficially false; at a deeper and more significant level they were legitimate and true.

The resurrection of Jesus is a different matter entirely. Its historicity is absolutely required for the Catholic religion to make any sense whatsoever. The Apostle Paul is, of course, forthright about the importance of Jesus' actual resurrection.

If Christ be not risen, then is our preaching vain, and **your faith is also vain.** Yea, and we are found false witnesses of God; because we have testified of God that he raised up Christ: whom he raised not up, if so be that the dead rise not. For if the dead rise not, then is not Christ raised: and **if Christ be not raised, your faith is vain**; ye are yet in your sins. Then they also which are fallen asleep in Christ are perished. **If in this life only we have hope in Christ, we are of all men most miserable.** [1Cor 15:14-24 KJV]

---

16 N. Kazantzakis "The Last Temptation of Christ" (1960)

To write this Paul must have himself believed in the historicity of this story: that it actually happened as an event in space-time. Now he never claims to be an eye-witness to the "empty tomb", though he was living in Jerusalem not long after the resurrection is supposed to have happened;[17] but he does claim to have had a miraculous encounter with the resurrected Christ[18] and to have later "compared notes" with other of the Apostles.[19]

It is not within the scope of this book to adduce all the reasons for believing that the resurrection narratives are not mythical; but it is important to ask the question: why would the Apostles make up such a story, knowing it to be untrue, and then be willing to die for it? They already had a serviceable religion, and some aspects of the New Testament were uncongenial to conventional Jewish sensibilities.

If Jesus' resurrection is a historic fact, this vindicates the whole Old Testament narrative – even if that narrative were to be proved entirely mythical. The Old Testament story would then be intelligible and valid as having been fabricated by human beings – under God's providential guidance and inspiration – to serve as the necessary overture, preparation and context for the Incarnation and Redemption.

I remember the film, "The Body",[20] and that the body turned out not to be Jesus after all. However, the protagonist did not know this and still had no reason to believe the body was not, in fact, Jesus. Yet he still had faith that in some way it wasn't true because… well, "just because" – or so it seemed. I found this unsettling because if physical evidence to the contrary is no impediment to faith then it seems to be a very ill-founded faith.

In the film "The Body" it was vital for the truth of the resurrection that the body in question was not that of Christ,

17 Acts 7:58-8:1; 22:20.
18 Acts 9:1-19.
19 Acts 9:26-27; 15:1-29.
20 J. McCord "The Body" (2001)

and this is how things turned out, of course. The body was in fact not any kind of "physical evidence to the contrary", it only *seemed* to be such. Evidence is always problematic. Corroboratory evidence is never adequate to validate a theory[21] and contrary evidence can only ever invalidate a theory in a particular theoretical context.

Moreover, evidence is very often not what it seems: which is one message that "The Body" is trying to put across. I remember watching an episode of the TV series "Kavanagh QC" in which it was clear beyond all reasonable doubt that a certain verdict was correct, the evidence supporting this verdict being overwhelming. At the end of the programme, once the verdict was given and the case was settled, one additional fact was revealed which entirely reversed the significance of the evidence presented to the court and meant that the verdict was wrong.

Only yesterday I watched another TV drama called "Witness for the Prosecution" in which overwhelming evidence of a man's innocence and of a woman's guilt was later shown to be entirely misleading. After seeing these two dramas I will be very loath to convict any-one if I am ever called to serve on a jury, as I am now convinced that no amount of evidence can exclude "reasonable doubt". Hence, no body of evidence can ever constitute proof or disproof, and all of our conclusions must be viewed as provisional, doubtful and subject to revision.

What the protagonist in "The Body" demonstrated was "faith". He continued to believe in the resurrection, in spite of the very strong circumstantial evidence to the contrary. It is important to recognise that he was correct to do so: both because his conclusion happened to be true, and because his faithfulness was a virtue to be admired rather than a naïvety to be disparaged. His faith was based both on his life-long experience of how believing in the resurrection had made sense of his existence, and had given a solid basis to ethics, and also on the testimony of the Apostles, as documented in the New Testament. It was neither blind nor founded on sentiment, as you insinuate.

---

21 K.R. Popper "The Logic of Scientific Discovery" (1980)

Cain's Complaint[22]

"My grain is golden ripe and good.
From it a wholesome flour I'll grind
with my mill stone
and many a crusty loaf of bread
and crumbly scone
I'll bake."

"I'll lay them out, as covenantal oath,[23]
before your altar, showing forth[24]
– and so proclaim –
Your grace towards Your favour'd folk;
and Your great fame
uphold."

"Why does not my oblation win regard?
Do You want of your people blood,
or smoking fat?
Is sudden death of some dumb beast
Your sick pleasure
or sport?"

"If bloody sacrifice is Your demand,
then how can I, who till the land,
and have not blood
to spare, aspire to please? Must I
mine own life's flood
now spill?
What offering can I make that's proper?

---

22 First published in "A Sparrow Falls" [S.C. Lovatt (2014)]
23 Gen 14:18. Lev 23:10-13.
24 The "shew-bread" or "Loaves of the Presence" of the Aaronic liturgy.
[Ex 25:30. 1Sam 21:6. 1Kgs 7:48. 1Chr 9:32. 2Chr 2:4; 13:11; 29:18.
Neh 10:33. Mat 12:4. Heb 9:2.]

Whatever gift to You I proffer,
is not mine; for
all's Yours, and I may do no more
than it restore
to You."

"If unaccountably You did require
some part of Earth's good store,
You have the rule
and right and might; so why demand
I play the role
of priest?"

[God's reply to Cain]

"Is winning my affection your desire?
There is no need to cool my ire
(that is: propitiation)
or bid (from fear of being overlooked)
for My attention
by gifts."

"There is no call for sibling rivalry.
Your brother's off'ring caught my eye
for it does signify
how My dear Son will shed His blood
and freely die,
for you;

and yet the rite I will inaugurate
your gift does close insinuate:
the fraction of a loaf,
the pouring out of ruby wine:
will be enough
memorial."[25]

"You're made worthy of My consideration
not by any oblation
(although of good intent,
and I commend the gift – as yours,
so be content
in that!)

but more by acting well and doing right;[26]
and also know with clear foresight
that when you fail,
you must not despair and wallow
in guilt and wail:
but rise

and hasten to the narrow crack
which is my means to have you back
where already lying
you'll find attentive to your call
a full off'ring
for sin."[27]

---

25 The Greek "amnemesis" (generally translated as "memorial") is a
   sacrificial word which means "that which serves to remind the
   Heavens of" either the person making the oblation or else a
   covenanted promise previously made to them. The Latin word
   "sacrament" has a similar implication, meaning an oath which binds
   God in an allegiance to humanity.
26 "If you do well, will you not be accepted?" [Gen 4:7. RSV]
27 The Hebrew which is normally translated as: "sin lieth at the door.
   And unto thee shall be his desire, and thou shalt rule over him,"
   [Gen 4:7. KJV] can also be rendered: "a sin-offering is laid-out
   at the opening. He shall desire you, and you shall command Him."

The Church is evil

The amount of ill-will and wickedness exhibited by the hierarchy of the Catholic Church leads me to think that religious institutions always do more harm than good.

It is sad that anyone should feel this way. I understand the basis for such feelings, of course. The Catholic hierarchy seems to have been focussed on undermining its own authority over my lifetime. The scandal associated with pederast clergy, the support for the "Magdalene Laundries" well into the late Twentieth Century, and the continued vilification and persecution of homosexuals are only three of the worst issues of interest to the secular media. The way in which Traditionalist Catholics were persecuted during the pontificates of Paul VI and Jon-Paul II also showed great ill-will.

> At times one gets the impression that our society needs to have at least one group to which no tolerance may be shown; which one can easily attack and hate. And should someone dare to approach them… he too loses any right to tolerance; he too can be treated hatefully, without misgiving or restraint. [Benedict XVI "Remission of the excommunication of the bishops of the Priestly Society of St Pius Xth" (2009)]

It isn't as simple as this, of course. The Church has done – and still does – a great deal of good, when it is not engaged in the "disturbed… self-criticism, you might even say self-destruction"[1] which has been central to its existence since the 1960's, and when it stops obsessing over sexual issues. There are lay-folk, religious, deacons, priests and bishops who are wise, humble, kind and gentle, as well as those who are foolish, haughty, ignorant and hateful. It is wrong to dismiss those who are good as unrepresentative, just as it is wrong to assert that those who are bad are typical, and indicative of the effect of organised religion.

---

1   Paul VI "Address to the Lombard College" (1968)

The Church is outwardly in the hands of narrow-minded self-righteous bigots: popes, bishops, some (but by no means all) priests, very many of the laity – and the rich well-connected laity at that – and these folks are not at all interested in transforming society in the direction of fairness, equity and justice for historically oppressed, subjugated, marginalized groups, such as women, homosexuals and (thank God now to a lesser extent, but the matter has hardly disappeared) people of colour.

However, I want you very much to know that for many of us, it is indeed precisely because we are Catholic Christians that we care about these matters, and that we do what we can to transform society for the better. [Private Communication form a friend]

Catholics are miserable

True religion ought to make people happy.
Catholicism doesn't make people happy.
Hence Catholicism is not true.

This syllogism is not valid, but it is significant in spite of this. Although it is not obviously true that "the true religion ought to make people happy," it is true that Catholicism claims to be "good news",[1] and to also give "peace... not as the world giveth."[2] Hence although the major premise is not sound, it is sound enough to serve while judging the truth of Catholicism, as long as "happiness" is understood more in terms of a deep tranquillity than a superficial jollity.

The assertion that "Catholicism doesn't make people happy," is less solid. In particular, it happens to be the case that there are significant aspects of my own life as a Catholic, and of my practice of Catholicism, which I find to be both very enjoyable and also rewarding in terms of perceived psychological benefit. I am sure that the same is true for many other Catholics. It is only necessary to read the writings of various saints to perceive that practising the Catholic Faith with integrity and commitment can be a source of great joy. It is also true that there are prominent aspects of the modern Catholic Church which I find repugnant and hateful; which cause me aggravation, grief and sorrow; and of which I am ashamed.

The way in which Catholicism mitigates people's "happiness" is often via feelings of guilt. This issue has two sides to it. On the one hand, when a person habitually acts contrary to justice it is not right that they be happy; rather, it is right and proper that they should be unhappy about their conduct. Hence it is no argument against the truth of any belief system that adhering to it makes some people unhappy about themselves. Perhaps they

---

1 Mat 4:23; 11:5; 24:14; 26:13. Mk 1:1, 14; 8:35; 13:10; 14:9; 16:15. Lk 2:10; 4:18,43; 7:22. Acts 8:11; 10:36; 13:32; 14:15. Heb 4:2-6. 1Pet 1:12, 25.
2 Jn 14:27. KJV

ought to feel that way, and the fact that the belief system is having this effect is evidential of its truth, not its falsity. On the other hand, it is easy to make people feel guilty when they have done nothing wrong. This is a powerful tool by which an authority figure can manipulate people into behaving to the advantage of that authority figure. It is very clear to me that this ploy is sometimes used by religious leaders (and also by "Charities" and commercial organizations) to advance their own ends. It is equally clear that this is the basis of "peer pressure", with its impetus to "conform" or else feel "wrong" or "unworthy".

Manipulating people by stirring up feelings of irrational inadequacy or guilt within them is wicked. The fact that some clerics and hierarchs do this is not surprising, given human nature. It is a serious embarrassment to the Catholic Church when its leaders act in this abusive way; however it is not evidence of the falsity of Catholicism, but only of the truth of the Catholic doctrine of "Original Sin" and its inevitable consequence "concupiscence."

Ritual does nothing for me

I don't find that religious ceremonies have any relevance to my life.

I can readily understand anyone saying that they find the worship style typical of modern Catholicism to be empty of meaning and significance, and of no relevance to their lives. I will make no attempt to defend the Mass of Paul VI, or any of the liturgical changes made to Roman Catholic ritual in the Twentieth Century.[1] I think that these changes did a lot to make Liturgy irrelevant to people. Hence very many stopped attending Mass.

Nevertheless, it is clear that human beings value ritual. Even secularists employ ritual from time to time, though they often disguise it in one way or another. People want to mark significant moments in their lives – birth, graduation, moving home, becoming blood-brothers, engagement, marriage, death, national days, inaugurations – by ritual acts. Ritual is how human beings express the conviction that some thing or person is important and worthy of attention. It is also how they afford this thing or person the attention which they believe to be appropriate.

To appreciate and obtain value from a ritual it is necessary to understand its significance. There is no point at all in going through some sequence of actions and enunciating some text in the absence of any understanding of what these actions and words are supposed to signify. It is absolutely necessary to be informed of the meaning of a ritual for it to have any possibility of "relevance".

Moreover, the criterion of "relevance" is suspect. When it comes to some Catholic ritual it can be argued that the ritual should be understood as the focus of ones life, and the question is more "is my life in conformance with what this ritual signifies?" than "is this ritual relevant to my life as it is now lived?"

---

1   S.C. Lovatt "In Reverence and Awe" (2014)

Those Catholic rituals which embody sacraments are a very special case. They do not simply symbolise supposed truths and do not simply serve to educate or inform,[2] but are supposed to be profoundly relevant to life as objective sources of divine help to live humanely and justly. Nothing could possibly be more "relevant" than the sacraments. In as far as you do not find the Most Holy Eucharist "relevant" this is a defect within yourself (not necessarily one that involves your culpability) and not an argument contrary to the worth of Catholic ritual. The correct response is to engage more actively with the ritual and try harder both to penetrate it and also be penetrated by it.

Finally, unless there is an intimate and personal basis to a person's religion, ritual is bound to be seen as purely formal and mechanical. The correct way to understand ritual is in terms of drama, poetry, wooing, flirting, courtship and love-making. Viewed this way, Holy Communion is an intensely erotic experience; though devoid of any genital excitement.

Lots of Catholics feel that the repetition of the same words and actions every at every Sunday Mass is boring. I say, not only do I find such repetition restful and beautiful, but also it is the heart of true liturgy. We require that repetition, that stability.

Look, it does not matter how we feel at Mass. We do not go to Mass in order to feel good. That is important, so I shall repeat it: We do not go to Mass in order to feel good. If you are bored, tough. We are all bored at one point or another.

Mass is not a concert, it is not a performance, it is not a sound-and-light show, it is not Star Wars. It is Reality, the truth of Philanthropia, God's love for us. Maybe we are allowed to glimpse it – and that indeed happens to some of us, rarely – but that is only a special favour, for people in need. For the great majority of us, Mass is a mixed bag: moments of rest, moments of concentration,

2   In a spiritual or psychological sense, not simply a factual, technical or intellectual sense.

moments of toil, moments of boredom, moments of distraction. Many moments of distraction – and that is OK, God has no problem with that, nor should we.

We do not go to Mass, once again, in order to seek pleasure. We go to Mass, because we love God, and we trust that somehow this action of ours serves God's will in the world: and that is our great consolation and encouragement.
[Private Communication from a friend]

I go to Mass because I experience something not of this world. To sit there and participate at Mass and knowing this is how heaven worships. By just reading the book of Revelation you see the similar things. Then, to receive Jesus Christ in the sacrament. That strength to go through anything. I recall the words of Christ who said that "Unless you eat the flesh and drink the blood of the Son of Man, you will not have life in you."[3]
[Private Communication from a friend]

---

3   Jn 6:53. RSV

I have not experienced God

I have never had any kind of personal religious or spiritual experience. I do not understand what it might mean "to have a personal relationship with God."

The first part of your statement is not important. The vast majority of religious or spiritual experiences can, rightly or wrongly, readily be dismissed as psychotic episodes. Schizophrenics regularly hear voices, have visions and see signs demanding their attention. I do not mean to say that all locutions, visions and signs are delusional. I only mean to say that they are not a proper foundation for faith. People who have had such experiences can lapse from faith in spite of having had the experience.

Moreover the first statement may not in fact be true. Sometimes one does not notice when a miracle happens. When you were visiting me last[1] I found myself in a dilemma as to where to take you to Church on Sunday. It seemed that all the convenient options were bad options, and that the only decent option was to hire a car and drive to the Birmingham Oratory. Even so, I had decided not to do that and somehow felt at peace with this decision. I remember feeling that "it would be OK" one way or another.

In the end — out of the blue, and without being asked — a friend, as you know, decided that he would like to go to the Birmingham Oratory himself, and also that he would like to visit us the same weekend that you were staying: so we were all able to go in his car. Now this was not a major miracle, but it did strike me as remarkable and providential; so perhaps this ought to count as falsifying your assertion. "Religious experiences" come in a wide range of forms, and this story certainly has the right kind of shape to have been a minor miracle.

---

1   Third Sunday of Advent, 2016.

The second part of your statement is very important and – I suspect – goes right to the heart of the matter. Given that a "personal relationship" is personal, it is rather difficult to speak of this dispassionately or analytically. I would first refer you to "The Cloud of Unknowing", then to Psalms (Vulgate numbering) 118, 22, 18, 12, 27, 32, 41, 62, 85, 102 and 138.

Plato puts the matter this way:

"So when someone rises by these stages, through loving boys correctly, and begins to see this beauty, he has almost grasped his goal… one goes always upwards, for the sake of this beauty: starting out from beautiful things… to all beautiful bodies, then… to beautiful customs… to learning beautiful things… and from these lessons he arrives in the end at this lesson, which is learning of this very Beauty, so that in the end he comes to know just what it is to be beautiful…

But what… if man had eyes to see true beauty - divine beauty, I mean, pure and dear and unalloyed, not clogged with the pollutions of mortality and all the colours and vanities of human life - thither looking, and **holding converse** with true beauty simple and divine? Do you think it would be a poor life for a human being to look there and to behold it by that which he ought, and **be with it**? Remember how… in that **communion** only, beholding beauty with the eye of the soul, he will be enabled to bring forth, not images of beauty, but realities (for he **has hold** not of an image but of a reality), and bringing forth and nourishing true virtue to **become the friend of God and be immortal**, if mortal man may."
[Ploto "Symposium" (211c-212a)]

Abraham and Moses and Jeremiah were all accustomed to addressing God in a very unguarded and direct – even challenging – way.[2] Abraham and Moses are both described

---

2   Gen 18. Ex 32:7-14, 30-33; 33:9-11.
    Jer 12:1-4; 14:19-22; 15:15-18; 18:19-23; 20:14-18.

as a "friend of God".[3] The attitude they had towards God can also be seen in the protagonist of the film "Priest".[4] Jesus teaches us to adopt the same direct and informal mode in the prayer which He taught His disciples.

When one really believes the Gospel – when one really believes that God is actually real, and is just and benevolent and kind and beautiful, and that God has gone to ridiculous lengths (including accepting ignominy and death) to rescue us humans from our best endeavours to ruin ourselves[5] – one cannot help but love God, and especially Jesus.

Having a "personal relationship with God" at root means being in love with God, on the basis of a deep understanding that God is all that we can possibly desire in terms of securing our life and abiding happiness. Having a "personal relationship with God" is nothing other than having the three theological virtues: "faith", "hope" and "charity". It is also called "being in a state of grace", and this is more typical Catholic terminology.

Faith is an intellectual commitment to the truths of the Catholic religion. Faith is dispassionate and theoretical. Faith is vital nevertheless, because apart from faith the other theological virtues are impossible; but faith is far from "sufficient" for salvation – contrary to what Luther asserted.

Hope is a person's acceptance that these truths relate to themselves; that they are not just abstract and theoretical, but rather concrete and personally applicable in practice. Hence for a human being to have hope in addition to faith, they must accept not just that "God is Love" and that "God is loving", but also that God loves them as a specific individual; and that because of this their own life has a security, solidity, robustness and wholeness which it would otherwise not possess of its own right.

---

3   Ex 33:11. 2Chr 20:7. Is 41:8. Js 2:23.
4   A. Bird & J. McGovern "Priest" (1994)
5   "God so loved the world, that He gave His only begotten Son, that whosoever believeth in Him should not perish, but have everlasting life." [Jn 3:16 KJV]

Hope is tied-up with an acknowledgement of one's own worthiness (in potential) of God's love: in spite of ones foolishness, weakness, and even wickedness. Often in Protestant thought faith and hope are conflated into one, and this combination is called "faith", but it is easy to distinguish them.

The Apostle James remarks that the devils believe that God is real, but that this faith does them no good[6] – as they don't have any hope in God. The devils are convinced that they must exist in opposition to God rather than in fellowship and communion with God.

Charity is a person's response to having gained hope. It is directed first towards God in joyous celebration of what hope means. This love is the purest and highest kind of Eros. It is then directed towards their neighbour, as it becomes apparent that the best way to express ones devotion to God and gratitude for what God has done – and promises to do – is to act justly and with kindness and consideration towards everyone that one meets. This love is "friendship" and – according to Plato – is only different from Eros in degree of intensity.[7]

We are told that "God is Love,"[8] so to have this theological virtue is to "share in the divine nature"[9] and be caught up in the interior (ecstatic, erotic and joyous) life of the Holy Trinity.

---

6   Jas 2:19.
7   Plato "Laws" 8:837a
8   1Jn 4:16.
9   2Pet 1:4.

I am afraid to go astray from God.

In this, I am speaking of *my* God,
of whom or what
ever had helped guided and saved me as a child
from a very dark, bad place
and people.

This God that I spoke to,
and that I still speak to,
I know in a very personal way,
as one might know a friend:
though in another sense
He seems unknowable in complete understanding.

He, I love and need dearly
and I want and need Him more than my life itself.
Though I am not certain that He,
that my Friend,
is the same that they speak of
in churches I have gone to
in search of kindred family
who were supposed to know Him too.

In this,
in speaking to you,
I am in hope of finding my family.
That perhaps you know of this Friend of mine too.

[Private Communication from a friend (Jan 2017)

Faith is an adjunct of fear

While I was a practising Catholic, my main motivation for belief and conformance to Catholic norms was a dread of possible damnation. I thought that the chance that I might finish up in Hell was a sufficient reason for "playing it safe" and going along with Catholicism. I now see that this was silly. Any-one can say "do such-and-such or risk being damned." That is no reason for paying any attention to what they say.

"Fear of Hell" is a very silly motive for practising Catholicism. It has never been a part of my reasons for being a Catholic. The proper motivation for practising the Catholic religion is love of God, and this comes back to the matter of a "personal relationship" with God.

I find it somewhat strange that this was ever a significant part of your mentality. I can't believe that you heard much, if anything, about Hell from the clergy of the remorselessly Modernistical parish[1] which you have been involved with through almost all your life. While it is well known that the threat of damnation has been used by preachers of all varieties in the past (more often Protestant than Catholic, if the truth be told) nowadays one hardly ever hears the word "Hell" spoken by a priest. Every funeral mass is predicated on the idea that the deceased – no matter how lapsed, atheistic, or even downright nasty – will get into Heaven, somehow or other.

This doesn't mean that the prospect of Hell is off the cards. I hope and pray that every soul will be saved, in accord with God's expressed will; but from my own experience with people it is clear to me that this is not a straight-forward matter. Some people are definitely Hell-bent in their Earthy lives, and it is difficult to see what would change their attitude in and for eternity: they are so committed to their way of looking at things – their prejudices and general perspective, their values,

---

1   St William of York, Forest Hill.

desires, vanities, preferences and expectations – that it would seem impossible for them to jettison these, even when shown that they are mistaken and harmful. I fear that if a cohort of angels were to argue the case for justice, beauty and love they would still reject it; and if God put in a personal appearance they would refuse to listen: asserting that God simply wants to undermine their autonomy and force their submission to divine diktat.

The only way to be sure of avoiding an eternity of alienation from all that is good and beautiful is to cleave to one's best intimation of what is good and beautiful in this passing life, and to become familiar with God's ways and purposes; and it is the central purpose of the Catholic religion to facilitate this: through beautiful ritual, architecture, music, and graphic art; the teaching contained in the Scriptures, the writings of the Fathers; the admonitions and instructions of the Magisterium; and the objective grace of the sacraments – though the post Vatican-II revolution has done a great deal to obscure this fact.

Satan's Story[2]

It's good to exist, even in this God-forsaken hole;
but, actually, that's not quite accurate:
Hell isn't so much forsaken as…
overlooked
purposefully overlooked.
One can't ever escape the Master of Puppets!
Not even here;
and you can be sure I've tried my best to escape
         that remorseless gaze.

The name's Satan:
on account of my having wandered
         the whole damnable world
in search of a place I could call my own.

All I want is some space to hang out in.
Not to be watched and monitored
         and evaluated and criticised all the time.
Not to be told what to do
         and what to think.
Some independence, you know:
autonomy.
Somewhere to chill,
and just be me.

It's not a lot to ask;
at least it doesn't
seem a big deal
to me.

---

2 First published in "The Good of Being" (2012) and then
   "Testaments" (2016)

Eventually, I kind of got my own way.
I'm allowed this little patch of obscurity:
my kingdom.
It's peaceful here.
No-one to contradict me.
No-one to judge me.

Of course, it wasn't always this way.
In the beginning I was glorious:
"First-born of all Creatures" and "Prince of the Cosmos."
"Lucifer", the Light-Bearer,
I was.

In my naïvety I was happy
          to bask in the Divine Radiance,
like a song-bird soaking up the Sun's rays
          on a bright summer's day;
but then it dawned on me
I was trapped,
like a moth circling a candle-flame:
it was impossible to grasp
the unendurable source of illumination,
yet it was impossible to escape
its indisputable fascination.

Eventually,
I got my act together.
I told myself that if
I was ever going to discover myself,
          and to find out what
I was truly capable of,
I just had to get away.

I felt the bond which held me
          begin to loosen, and
I made my bid for freedom.
"Independence at last!" or so
I thought in my elation, as
I fled the celestial dazzle.

I pushed past startled throngs of angelic beings,
crying aloud my paean of liberty:
"To yourself be true!"
Others of the host gathered to my side
and joined my breakout.

Now we are here:
wanderers all.
Searching for a way to be
truly ourselves
and to be answerable
only to ourselves.
Liberty is too important to be sacrificed
on the altar of security and comfort!

I'm sure we did the right thing.
And yet… what is to become of us?
This place is no proper answer.
Our rebellion was only partly effective.
We escaped the divine immediacy, true;
but we have not escaped divine knowledge,
still less divine power.
I'm not stupid. I know full well
that all we are, and all that we do is dependent on the Maker.
How could it be otherwise?

Why did God let us go, then?
I'm sure that's what happened.
I'd not have been able to escape, if
I'd not been allowed to escape.
Am I the victim of some divine plot,
which even my towering intellect cannot fathom?

Will we ever be
truly free:
absolutely independent?
I fear not;
but perhaps we might just be able to negotiate some kind of
stand-off.
After all, why should God care about what you and I
get up to?
Surely He's got better things to occupy His mind!

All I long for is justice:
a possibility for fulfilment
of myself
on my own terms,
not dictated or infringed on by another;
not even by One who claims to have
my best interest at heart.

Yet how can this be?
God will always be sovereign,
despite my best efforts.
I can never overthrow the Divine tyranny.

Perhaps the future is fixed, even now.
Perhaps I'm trapped and there's no escape.
Perhaps I'll have to admit defeat in the end,
        and sink back into those Everlasting Arms;
but for now
I stand resolute:
resolute and proud
in this comforting darkness.

The Church is fixated on sex

While I was a practising Catholic, I found the Church's attitude towards sex oppressive and a source of unproductive guilt which did not lead to any kind of change in my life. Now that I have given up on religion I feel liberated and free from guilt.

I think that the Church is obsessed with sex in an unhealthy way, and I do not buy into the generality of Catholic teaching on sex and gender. Indeed, I think that an awful lot of sex-based guilt is misplaced and destructive. In particular, I do not think that non-procreative sexual activity is wrong merely because it is non-procreative: hence solo masturbation, sexual activity other than vaginal intercourse, and contraceptive vaginal intercourse are not automatically wrong.

However, the facts that sexual activity is not naughty, dirty or shameful – and that sexual pleasure is no more sinful than any other bodily pleasure – do not mean that "anything goes between consenting adults" when it comes to sexual activity. General ethical issues about self-respect and respecting others, honesty, proportionality, prudence, habituation and addiction are all relevant.

Moreover, it is important to recognise that a state of sexual arousal is not conducive to dispassionate thought and calm decision making, hence it is important to habituate a sexual ethic (that is, "purity") and aesthetic (that is, "modesty") which substantiate and express these general principles in a manner that is relevant to the sexual dimension of ones life.

This is not the place to explore what "purity" and "modesty" might amount to on the basis I am indicating; though that task would surely be worthwhile. It will suffice to say that I suspect they would have some large commonality with the conventional understanding of these terms, but would nevertheless diverge significantly from them.

The fact that you now feel liberated and free from sexual guilt is both good and bad. In as far as this means that you have rejected Augustine's irrational evaluation of sex as being demeaning and dishonourable, this is good. In as far as it means that you have adopted a "permissive" – or even promiscuous – sexual ethic, then I cannot allow that this is good at all.

There are three ways to be freed of guilt. The first two are fine, the third is anything but fine.

1. To be forgiven for doing what was wrong.
2. To realise that you hadn't done anything wrong, and never should have felt guilty.
3. To convince yourself that some actual wrong you committed was not wrong after all.

What is the point of the Church?

I'm a scientist and a Christian. I grew up thinking that Evangelical doctrine was Christianity and that I had to put up with the things in it I didn't like if I wanted to be Christian. There was enough in Jesus that made me want to be a "follower" and put up with the rest.

Over the years I learnt (solely via your explanations and the books you have suggested I read) that Catholic theology is both "nicer" and more reasonable – so much so, that it is hard now for me to sit through Evangelical services – I guess my ears have become attuned to the underlying theology. Although I agree with Catholic theology as far as it relates to God and our status with God, I find that everything related to the role of the Church just speaks to me of maintaining a powerful, hierarchical institution, interested in its own survival above all else; with as much soul as a multinational corporation: which might at least pay me a decent salary for my time!

The less Evangelical Protestant churches tend to be, frankly, boring – as I have found Catholic services I've attended (sorry, but even more so the Tridentine one) So for some time I've stopped attending Church anywhere, and my thoughts are "Does it matter at all?" and "What is the point of Church?" and "Why do churches make attendance obligatory for all believers?"

The view of Jesus I get from the Bible and from my (Protestant) upbringing I find very appealing and He is someone I want to follow. The view I have of the Catholic Church is very different, and I have no desire to follow the Church. If at some point it seems the only way I can follow Jesus is to join a particular Church, then I'll do what I have to, I suppose.

The problem here is the phrase "The Church". The Church is not identifiable with any human organization. It is the Body of Christ, the Kingdom of God's friends. It exists perfectly in the Heart of God and there it is Holy and Spotless. It is only imperfectly realised in the human reality and organization that calls itself the Catholic Church.

I detest and despise much of the Contemporary Church, both its leadership and its culture. Nevertheless, I know that the authority of the Church (the whole Church Community, not just its hierarchy) is prior to that of the Scriptures.

> I have faith in Jesus and God, but have no faith in the Church. For someone to say that my faith is only human rather than divine (whatever that means: our faith is our own, and is either true or false. As all true things are from God so is true faith) is irrational and hubristic.

Faith is at root a gift from God and generally comes from an encounter with God in the testimony and lives of others. Faith is not a "good work", something that we originate, own and are personally responsible for. It is certainly not something that one obtains by a dutiful reading of the Bible.

It is easy for a conservative Catholic to argue: "Jesus couldn't possible inspire someone to have a real faith that did not involve a commitment to His visible body. Hence, it must be that anyone who professes faith in Jesus, but does not at least explicitly desire to belong to the Catholic Church cannot have a real faith!"

This argument is false. Faith isn't ever perfect. Whereas membership of the Catholic Church is an unavoidable consequence of a fully mature, developed, and authentic faith, it does not follow that only those who are visible members of the Catholic Church can have a real faith. We each perceive the object of faith imperfectly: as through a distorting and corroded mirror. We can only have ortho-doxa (true opinion), at best, and "being *in* good faith" doesn't guarantee "accuracy *of* faith".

> If I am to be told that my faith is meaningless and the choice is the Church or nothing, I choose nothing!

Quite right too! On the other hand, the true definition of "The Catholic Church" is the Community of God's Friends: those who are "in good faith" and, more importantly, have charity! Faith and Hope and Charity are not, at root, things that you and I generate: they are all elicited by God's grace. They are God's work, not ours; and in the end they will lead anyone who is sincere (perhaps kicking and screaming) to the Catholic Church. The problem is that the historical institutional Church is a very imperfect realization of the Ideal Church.

> The knowledge that any view I have of Jesus has been filtered by the Church, means that it is likely to be inaccurate, and to be the view that is necessary to keep the Church going. Nevertheless, I will hold onto my hope that I have a view of Jesus, who I would like to follow, that has been untainted by two thousand years of human history in the Church.

From where do you get this view, if not from the Church? The view we have of Jesus in the Gospels is derivative of the Church's viewpoint and agenda. How can you know that it is untainted?

I believe that Holy Spirit in fact acts through the Church to preserve the authentic message of Jesus. I entirely accept that this is something I believe by choice, and is an act of the will rather than something I can convincingly demonstrate by argument. Nevertheless, I think that it is a serviceable hypothesis.

> What did Jesus mean by the word "Church" when he said "upon this rock I build my Church, and the gates of Hell will not prevail against it"[1] when there was no such thing as a Church beforehand? It is hard to believe that by "Church" he meant what the Roman Church is now.

---

1 Mt 16:18.

What did Jesus institute and what have humans subsequently made of it? Maybe the first fifty years of early Christianity attracted this promise, and what we have now is a human institution, totally different from what He "built".

The word Jesus uses signifies "those who are 'called out' or 'gathered together'." Of course it means "a group of people", but beware of that dangerous word "just". It is vaguely equivalent to the words "society, folk, nation, community and congregation." It certainly does not mean "a bureaucratic or hierarchical institution." On the other hand it doesn't exclude the idea that "Jesus' People" would have to have a bureaucracy and hierarchy.

Regarding Jesus' promise that "The Gates of Hell will not prevail" against His Church, this sounds more like a promise that the power of evil to enslave people would certainly be broken, so that they will be free to join the Community of the Redeemed, rather than a promise that the bulk of the institutional Church will preserve the Apostolic Tradition to the End of Time.

Indeed, Jesus asks elsewhere: "When the Son of Man comes, will He find faith on Earth?"[2] with the apparent implication: "no!" He also says: "Most men's love will grow cold, but he who endures to the end will be saved."[3] Jesus seems to have envisaged his Church being reduced to a faithful few at the time that He returned in Glory. This view is favoured by traditionalist[4]

---

2   Lk 18:18. RSV

3   Mt 24:12-13. RSV

4   Those who accept and see themselves as participating in the handing on of the "deposit of faith" as taught by Christ and His Apostles. They believe that although the understanding of this faith becomes clearer and more sophisticated as time goes by, its basic content does not change, and that doctrine should not be adjusted so as to accord with contemporary ideas. They value continuity of practice and disparage change, believing that stability of expression and aesthetic is a powerful force in defence of orthodoxy. They typically deplore the the Liturgical Revolution instigated under the authority of Paul VI on the basis that it tended to the undermining of Catholic belief.

Catholics, and looked on askance by both conservatives[5] and liberals.[6]

> Is the Church for God or for us? It seems to me that since God is perfect and needs nothing for His own fulfilment, the only reason He can want something to happen in the world is because it is to the good of something else that He values: that is, us. If Church is supposed to be good for us, is there any point to going/joining in if it is not actually good for us?
>
> I guess the Church would argue that attendance at Mass is good for us, even if we ourselves can detect no benefit within ourselves. However, I prefer to be my own judge of what is good for me and someone else would have to win my trust before I would listen to them.

The Church is for us, and for our salvation: for exactly the reason you give. Obviously, there is no point in doing anything that is not good for us; but the content of this question is hidden in the word "good". One must consider what is objectively good for the

---

5 Those who think that the contemporary hierarchy should be respected, trusted and obeyed in all matters. These are the inheritors of the "Ultra-Montanist" party of the Nineteenth Century, who believed in a very extensive notion of papal infallibility and promoted the idea that the pope is an absolute monarch. They tend to assert that current papal policy and practice is always wise and in accord with tradition, even when it manifestly is not. They typically support the Liturgical Revolution instigated under the authority of Paul VI on the basis that it must have been a good idea because it was imposed by a pope.

6 Those who think that it is important to adjust doctrine to accord with contemporary ideas, that novelty is good in itself, and that the very idea of stable dogma is oppressive. These are the inheritors of the "Modernist" party of the early Twentieth Century, who believed exactly the same things. They support the Liturgical Revolution instigated under the authority of Paul VI on the basis that it resulted in a great disruption of Catholic belief. Moreover, they would like to see further disruption of liturgical practice.

individual. This is not the same as what they find agreeable, or of obvious immediate benefit.

Your point about winning trust is very important. A serious problem which the hierarchy must face – and as yet refuses to – is that it has lost the trust of vast numbers of people over the last fifty years. Many have deserted the pews in disgust or confusion. Others remain, but pay little attention any more to what the hierarchy says. The hierarchy has little taste for humble pie; but it will not gain the trust and respect of contemporary society until it repents of its high handedness and discredited policies.

> Is the Church's role to uphold orthodoxy? Why does it matter if people believe things that are not true? I think this only matters if it leads to harmful actions.

As Jesus said: "What you bind on Earth shall be bound in Heaven"[7] and "When the Spirit of truth comes, he will guide you into all the truth."[8] I agree that the only purpose of right belief is to facilitate and foster right behaviour. I believe, however, that any proposition which is true will have some practical implications. Objective reality simply has this effect. Sometimes this may only be by a double negative. The denial of a doctrine may, if followed through logically, require the adoption of some unexpected unpleasant attitude.

Also, there is a huge difference between "happening to differ from orthodoxy" and "being committed to a deviation from orthodoxy." The former is called "material heresy", which few – if any! – of us can entirely avoid. The latter is called "formal heresy", and is a serious matter indeed.

> Is the Church's role to distribute the sacraments, and in particular Holy Communion?

The Church doesn't exist because of the sacraments: they exist because of the Church. The sacraments only make sense in the context that is the Church. Arguably, the Church is itself the

---

7   Mt 16:19; 18:18.
8   Jn 16:13. RSV

greatest sacrament of all. If there was no community of disciples, but only individual believers, then there would be no purpose for anything like the Catholic sacraments.

> I can see two other takes on this. The last supper was a once-in-a-lifetime event for the disciples. So perhaps partaking of the body should really be a once-in-a-lifetime event. If we take in Jesus, why has He disappeared at the end of the next week/day? Alternatively, Jesus also said "as oft as you eat it, do so in remembrance of me." That to me conveys that whenever I eat a standard meal I should do so in remembrance of Jesus: and who needs a priest for that?

The important thing is not the "physical taking in" of Jesus, but the psycho-spiritual process: the intimate encounter with God. This encounter can, and should be, repeated as often as its recollection grows dim in our hearts. If our memories were as good as immediate experience, and we were never conscious of having sinned, then there would be no need to receive Holy Communion more than once in our whole life.

Some sacraments (those that relate to status in the Community: Baptism, Confirmation/Chrismation, Ordination and Marriage – between any one pair of individuals) are unrepeatable, for the reason implied by your question. Other sacraments (those that exist to nurture the spirituality of the individual within the Community: Holy Communion, Penance and Extreme Unction) can, and should be, repeated, at psycho-physiological need.

Remembering Jesus every time one has a meal is a worthy spiritual exercise, but is in no way to be identified with Holy Communion. We should each strive to live our life and conduct our work (not just eat our meals) recalling the presence of Jesus and as an offering to God.

All Christians are anointed priests in one sense: by virtue of their Baptism and Confirmation. We do not need any other appointed intermediary to address God for us. While we can, laudably, choose to ask someone else (for example a living friend or canonized saint) to intercede for us with God, it is quite right

and proper and normal for any Christian to confidently approach
God him or herself.

> I do have sympathy with the idea that it is good to have
> someone with the final word on matters of orthodoxy to
> stamp a "yes" or "no" on a disputed proposition as, unlike
> in science, there is generally no experimental test.

This is, of course, crucial.

> But why the rest of the paraphernalia? I guess I've found
> Catholic services I've been to rather tedious (even worse
> when in Latin) pretty much saying the same thing every
> week. Little interaction. Is this really how Jesus expects
> his followers to be spending their time? Maybe if it
> revitalizes you to go out and live the life of integrity,
> to seek justice, to stand up for your beliefs or to be more
> loving and caring – but if not, what's the point?

This is one of your core difficulties, it seems to me. One finds
anything tedious which one doesn't see the point of, and when
one sees the point then what was previously tedious becomes full
of vitality. I know that much of my own response to the Old Latin
Ritual is conditioned by what it stands for. I am not opposed
to a more demonstrative style of worship;[9] however, it seems to
me that to evaluate a form of worship in terms of subjective
experience is to put the cart before the horse.

I am sure that this is not an insoluble problem for you.
The issue has to be dealt with experientially I think. You have
to first want it to work, perhaps. Some people are drawn to faith
by the liturgy: for others this is the last step. We are all different.
You will come to the Church, I expect, by a hard intellectual grind
and battle: kicking and screaming all the way. Not the most
pleasant experience for you, and not to be generally
recommended: but if I am right, it will be your way – and that will
make it right for you.

9 For example, I love the exuberant liturgy of the Ethiopian Orthodox
   Church.

I would say that Catholic worship has "revitalized" many folk "to go out and live the life of integrity, to seek justice, to stand up for their beliefs, or to be more loving and caring." Such folk are generally called "canonized saints." Obviously, other forms of religious observance may be thought to have had similar effects on other folk. My point is that one finds "new life" in one's personal encounter with They-Who-Is-Love. This happens primarily in the secret places of one's own heart. Worship is a corporate effort to nurture, manifest and make space for this process. Better: it is the response of the community to the vocation of God. Better still: it is the transcendent action of that vocation within the community.

Worship should not be viewed as performance: what we do towards God; still less entertainment: what we do towards each other; or therapy: what we do for each other; but as sacramental: what God does towards us. Our response may be meagre. Perhaps reserve and understatement are called for, in order to emphasize the immediate action of God hidden within the Action of the Mass. Perhaps the austere Roman way is superior to the exuberance of the Goth, Byzantine, Syrian and Copt.

> I do believe we all have a need for community. Even the loners, who I think become so out of despair of ever meeting someone they can or dare trust.

That is a very beautiful, though frightening, thought!

> No Catholic church I've been to appears to be a community. I assume monasteries are real communities, but have no experience of such.

This is more or less my experience, too. Parishes vary from being factional and cliquey to down-right cold and hostile. The first parish that I attended in Harrow for a time was a bit better: but that was largely because I was involved in the charismatic prayer group there. Similarly, the parish I attended in Leigh-on-Sea: but that was because I got myself onto the Parish Council for a time and get involved in a Parish visitation/mission exercise.

I also believe we all have a need to worship something
higher than ourselves. I take a Platonic viewpoint, in
thinking we all have some notion of the perfect form of
anything – including being human – and when we do not
see perfection (and certainly not within ourselves) we
wish to affirm that such a perfect form does subsist
somewhere. It is often misplaced onto other mere humans
(being in-love, hero-worship, and so on) which leads to
disillusionment when flaws are found. It is good for an
institution to direct such worship at the one true and only
person worthy of such: Jesus.

This is very well said. I wish to add nothing.

The group is stronger than the individual. If like-minded
individuals join together with a common goal, then they
can achieve much more than alone.

Unfortunately, this requires wise leadership and an openness to
grass-roots initiatives. Both are rare in the Catholic Church today.

When Church does not form the community, then
something else will play this role, with other objectives:
for example corporations, whose goal is financial profit.

This is more important than it sounds.

Is the goal of Church to transform the world?
Is the Church necessary for this?

This is the defining vocation of the Church. This work will never
be completed, but it is the business of the Church to work for
Universal Justice. This is at least part of the point of the parables
of "the leaven in the dough," "the savourless salt," "the city on a
hill," and "the lamp that should not be hidden."[10] The Kingdom
of God is at hand and is supposed to be breaking out all over.[11]

---

10 Mt 5:13-16.
11 Mt 3:2; 4:17; 10:7; 12:28. Mk 1:15. Lk 10:9-11; 11:20; 17:21.

> Is the goal of Church to share the Gospel? Does this lead
> to the former?

This is the same activity. Proclaiming the Gospel means campaigning for the establishment of the Kingdom. Authentic evangelism necessarily results in the coming of the Kingdom. It changes people's lives.

> Is the goal of Church to bring more people to Heaven?

Certainly to make the process easier and less painful. Whether the total number is increased is not for us to say.

> Is the goal of Church to provide a refuge for the lonely,
> the poor and the downtrodden?

This is part of the core business of the Kingdom. Jesus made that obvious at every turn.

> Does participation in the Church make anyone think they
> are achieving more towards any of these goals than if they
> did not participate?

I think you are confusing "participation in the Church" with "playing a formal role in the organized community." As you are well aware, I generally avoid the latter: limiting my overtly Catholic activity to Sunday and Holiday Mass attendance. Whereas my involvement in the activity of the Catholic Church should be a cause of inspiration, sadly it is not. In practice it is a cause for desperation.

Similarly, my membership of the Catholic Church should provide me with a network through which I could operate for the good of the whole; but in fact I find that my membership of the Catholic Church acts to limit what I can do: because I am sure that if I did much more than I do do, I would attract the attention and condemnation of the New Order hierarchy.

Nevertheless, my consciousness of being a Catholic, of being part of that historic spiritual tradition that goes back to the Fathers of the Church and its founding Apostles (I exclude Jesus from this list as being an altogether different category of person) and before them, on the one hand to Plato and Pythagorus, and on the other hand to Ezekiel, Elijah, Samuel, David, Moses, Jacob, Melchizidek, Abraham, Noah, Enoch and Adam is a great inspiration and comfort to me.

More than this, being a Catholic means being a member of the Mystical Body of Christ and a friend of God. This gives me a basis for hope that it is worth-while doing things which seem pointless from a human perspective.

Possible reasons for Church attendance

> **Holy Communion:** "Receiving Jesus" as often as possible. If this "intimacy with Jesus" is so amazing and the role of the Church is to pass it out, then it is despicable that the Church would ever withhold the sacrament from those who wish to receive it – so excommunication should never happen and non Catholics should be able to receive. The withholding of something that God has entrusted the Church to distribute, from those who do not toe the party line suggests the Church cares mostly about maintaining its political power.

This is an emotive issue and difficult to discuss dispassionately. What I must do is show that while Holy Communion is every bit as significant as you indicate,[12,13] its physical reception is not absolutely necessary, that taking communion can sometimes be counterproductive, and that refraining from taking communion can be a means of grace.[14] I address both of these issue later on.

---

12 I write at length of "The Holy Eucharist" in my book "In Reverence and Awe" (2016)

13 See page 107.

14 See pages 110–114.

Teaching: keeping our thoughts from straying away from orthodoxy and reminding us what we ought to believe; but this rather suggests to me that somebody who cares about theology should read the Catholic texts.

You are right here, but the public reading of Scripture and exposition of its meaning has always been part of Judeo-Christianity. It is a way of bringing to mind and celebrating the facts of Salvation History. Of course, an ill-informed or perfunctory exposition will achieve the opposite result.

The culture: help us to feel that those beliefs are OK and reasonable. I think this is related to community. Being among those who believe in similar things makes one more confident that it is OK. It affirms and makes one more courageous in ones beliefs.

I agree with what you say here. I suppose you feel this especially keenly, now that you have ceased attending formal worship.

The people: provide companionship and even friendship with like-minded. Great, if this is true.

Once more, I agree with what you say here – including, sadly, the implications of your final caveat!

Endeavours: enable our energy to be channelled into actions aligned with our goal via an appropriate organization which is already set up, so that we achieve more than we could alone. Great, if this is true.

Once more, I agree with what you say here – including, sadly, the implications of your final caveat!

> **Supporting God's institution:** even if it does us or
> nobody else any good right now, over history it's survival
> is vital for human well-being, both in this world and in
> order for many to reach the hereafter. A good reason, but a
> bit too long-term for most people, and if this is your only
> reason, your dedication is worthy of a Saint!

It is difficult to see how an institution that in fact does no-one any
good here and now could ever serve such a purpose in the future.
I suppose you mean that there is always the hope that good people
will eventually regain control of the levers of power, and I
suppose you are right. Certainly this has happened in the past.
The resurgence of the Roman Church in response to the challenge
of Luther and Calvin is a prime example of this.

You are again confusing the Ideal Form of the Catholic
Church of Christ (to which it is absolutely necessary to belong
in order to be saved: because to be saved is the same condition
as to participate in this Form) with its present exemplification and,
in particular, its leadership. I cannot emphasize enough that "The
Church" is not the same as the hierarchy any more than
"Apostolic Tradition" is the same as the magisterium.

> **Supporting the hierarchy:** maintaining the financial and
> political power of the institution. For me, a reason not to
> go as I dislike hierarchies!

The difficulty with institutional power is its abuse, not its
existence. Given the existence of a large community, some form
of hierarchy is more or less inevitable. Moses tried to manage
without it when he led the Hebrews out of Egypt, but gave
in to the inevitable when told off by Jethro, Priest of Midean.[15]

---

15 Ex18:14-26.

Problems with transubstantiation

I am not sure what to make of transubstantiation.[12]

You make this very obvious. On the one hand you argue from the basis that Holy Communion is incredibly important and because of this should be available to all who desire to receive it. On the other hand you argue that Holy Communion is no more than the eating of common-place food, and so does not require the agency of any ministerial priesthood.[12]

Either that is Jesus they are holding up in front of people during the service or it is not. I don't think it is Jesus...

At the Last Supper, Jesus said privately to his Apostles: "This is My Body" and "This is My Blood" (not "this represents my body and my blood.") He had previously set the context for this startling announcement with extended, stark and uncompromising public teaching.[16] St Paul describes the Sacrament as being a participation in the Body and Blood of Christ.[17] He bolsters this strong statement of Platonic theory with a clear practical warning that to receive the sacrament unworthily is to risk physical sickness, and even death.[18]

The early Fathers are mostly clear that the Eucharistic Elements are not just symbols: though their testimony is complicated by the fact that they are symbols (just not just symbols) and sometimes they talk about what they symbolize.[12] They do not use the medieval language of transubstantiation simply because they are generally Platonists not Aristotelians and such terminology would have been entirely foreign to them.[12] The East has never adopted this language but has no less a developed view of the numinousity and objective sanctity of the Blessed Sacrament than the West.

---

16 Jn 6.
17 1Cor 10:16.
18 1Cor 11:30.

> (and in fact every single Catholic I have asked this
> question to – I guess about a half dozen, not including my
> wife's immediate family, who I am sure would give the
> same answer – have said, "no it is just a symbol")

This shows you just how terrible the position within Catholicism
is today. It shouldn't need to be said that any person who says
"Holy Communion or the Blessed Sacrament is just a symbol"
by that fact makes themselves a material heretic as it is a direct
denial of the infallible teaching of the Council of Trent.

> I don't think it is true; but like in a good novel, the actions
> of some characters in the novel (and those characters
> really do themselves believe their actions to be real)
> can still make you shudder. So, the whole process of
> transubstantiation… I can imagine it to be true, in the way
> I that can imagine a real live encounter with Jesus every
> week, which would be a wonderful thing…

You understand what the point of Holy Communion would be,
if only it were to be true. That's one thing that I don't have
to explain to you. Note that the "Catholics" you have spoken
to probably wouldn't agree with you on this!

> …unlike my own experience of communion…

You regularly put too much emphasis on subjective experience.
Sometimes I find receiving Holy Communion to be deeply
moving and inspiring. Sometimes I find it a "non-event". Neither
experience proves anything at all. People are good at generating
imaginary religious experiences.

Thomas Aquinas gets this one spot on when he tells us that
the sense impressions and subjective experience associated with
the Blessed Sacrament are of no account or significance
whatsoever. All that matters is what Jesus said: "This is my body.
This is my blood." We must simply believe what He says,
seek to understand it[12] and thank our ardent Lord for the great

and precious gift of intimacy which He offers us as an eternal pledge of his love for us.

> ...this seems like something the hierarchy implants in people's minds, then uses as a control device.

Not a very good control device, given all the loop-holes. Your criticism is much better directed at the sacrament of Penance, in this case I am sure that you are correct; but only under the practice of the sacrament as popularised over the last few hundred years, and which has now virtually died out.

> It would have exactly the same effect as getting people a physical brain implant when young, and controlling the release of drug on a weekly basis, and telling them that if they do not agree with the hierarchy's policy they will get no more drug. The sad thing is the drug only works on the real believers: who the majority might say are fools for going along with the whole process, but are the ones I find I have most sympathy for – as they are the ones who are most looking beyond this world to the next.

Up to a point, but I think you are confusing "real believers" with "those who tend to do what they are told without question." These are not at all the same sets of people. What you are describing here is an abuse of the sacrament, not authentic purpose.

> It seems abominable to me for anyone to prevent someone from following what they believe to be Jesus' command, or to deny them their "intimacy with God" on the basis of power politics about moral issues. I am angry when I hear the hierarchy say they will withhold Communion from real Catholics who vote to allow gay marriage and so on. The image in my head is from the film "Priest", when the protagonist withheld communion from his lover. To me it seems a direct contradiction of Jesus' statements "ask and you will receive"[19] and "him who comes to me I will not

---

19 Mt 21:22. Jn 16:24.

cast out."[20] The idea that the Church really does have
Jesus, and is preventing people coming and receiving Him
is… well, that is the most controlling, uncaring, and
hypocritical action I can think of!

As you put this, you are correct. I am pretty sure that Jesus would
have given Holy Communion to Judas at the Last Supper,
if he hadn't left early. However, you are being too emotive and
not analytical enough.

Right and wrong use of excommunication

It is quite wrong for the hierarchy to use excommunication – still
more "interdict", where all the sacraments are withdrawn from the
population of an entire country in order to put the State under
pressure – as a lever in "power politics", either with rulers
or legislators. This hasn't stopped popes from doing exactly this
in the past. I am not answerable for the actions of vindictive men.
Neither is it needful to excuse the misuse of a power for its
legitimate exercise to be recognized.

As to whether excommunication is a valid response to "moral
issues", it seems to me that it could well be. For example, I think
that it would be quite proper for unrepentant pederast priests
(and those Bishops who connived to conceal their activities,
and who still refuse to admit their fault and retire from office)
to be excommunicated. Similarly the leaders and active
membership of terrorist organizations such as the IRA, ETA
and PLO. What should be done if some notoriously wicked person
presents themselves for Holy Communion? If they are allowed
to receive communion it would quite fairly be taken as a degree
of approval or acquiescence in their actions. This is not right.
It would be a cause of grave scandal.

In the last analysis, it is legitimate for the hierarchy to insist
that Catholic legislators vote in a particular way on a particular
issue, under pain of excommunication; but this would generally
be an unwise and counter-productive course of action. It would

---

20 Jn 6:37. RSV

open all Catholic politicians to the charge that they were mere puppets of the Vatican, and would bring the Church into disrepute. Nevertheless, in a case of perceived extreme gravity (such as abortion, slavery, female genital mutilation, usury, divorce, adultery, polygamy, euthanasia, cloning, the right to worship, the right to evangelise, or homosexual marriage) it might be prudent for the hierarchy to accept this political cost in order to maintain an objective and principled stance.

> If the sacrament was so important, they would never withhold it form anyone; so I can only think that the Church does not see it really as that important for the recipient, but rather something it can use to maintain its power: i.e. you have to do X because it is good for you, but if you disagree with us about other things, we will not let you take part in wonderful X. This makes me angry.

This anger is understandable. You are denied Catholic Communion while believing much Catholic doctrine and accepting much of the Catholic vocation. Many others are admitted to Catholic Communion by the New Order hierarchy while notoriously rejecting core elements of the Tradition; positively espousing indifferentist, Masonic, or Protestant beliefs; or schismatic and synchretistic practices.

In practice, the Catholic Church cannot not prevent anyone from receiving Holy Communion. The most that the Catholic hierarchy can do is refuse to offer Communion to some (group of) person(s). Typically, anyone who is excommunicated has recourse to any number of other groupings: many of which have good claims to objectively valid sacraments. Moreover, it is generally possible for anyone to receive Catholic Communion. Anyone who presents themselves at the altar will almost inevitably be given Communion. Only if they are recognised as being a notorious sinner is there any possibility of their being refused.

In fact, some people are objectively not in communion with the Church. Others are in unrepented grave sin. These should not receive communion. They should be told this in no uncertain terms and the reasons made clear to them, if necessary. Even so, if a person believed by those in authority to be in such a state presents themselves to receive Communion, it will be given to them: first, because they may in fact not be in such a state, and should be given the benefit of the doubt; second, because even if they are in such a state, it might be thought better to give them Communion than hazard conflict at such a sacred moment, unless it is judged that the harm done by appearing to countenance their sin is worse.

Holy Communion is a great good for the individual, but not their greatest good

You try to argue that because something is a great good, it should never be withheld; and yet in doing so you disclose exactly what the Catholic doctrine is, while somewhat misrepresenting it. The Church believes that a person's subjective beliefs, attitudes, values and lifestyle are much more important than external actions – even sacramental actions: which are, after all, only meant to inform, inspire and strengthen these characteristics of their life. While it is true that the reception of a sacrament in good faith is an ordinary means of grace, St Paul warns that a person receiving Holy Communion unworthily risks further injury to themselves.[21]

A Bishop has a personal responsibility before Almighty God to warn individuals and groups when he believes that they are going off the rails. In the last analysis this warning must become public and formal. If it is rejected, then the Bishop has little choice but to withdraw his responsibility of oversight. This is for the good of the individual(s) being admonished and for the rest of the community who, hopefully, are thereby deterred from following a similar path. Of course, the Bishop might be mistaken in his judgement. This would be regrettable, but it does not make his judgement any the less binding for the time being: subject to appeal to Primate, Patriarch or Pope. A pious respect for lawful authority is necessary if peace and good order is to be maintained.

---

21 1Cor 11:27-32.

If some individual(s) happen to be wronged (as has, regrettably, often been the case) they will not be denied grace by God. Rather their exclusion from the ordinary means of grace will certainly become for them an extra-ordinary means of grace, if only they patiently bear the burden which they unjustly suffer. It is quite proper for such (an) individual(s) to protest that the judgement made against them was mistaken, as long as they do not deny the legitimacy of the office of that authority which has condemned them.

In particular, excommunication these days does not involve forbidding individuals from attending Catholic worship (it did so in the past) but only from physically receiving Communion. Hence it is a simple matter for anyone who is excommunicated to make a "spiritual communion" in the context of the community Eucharistic worship. This was in any case the common practice of 99% of laity in good standing on most Sundays throughout most of the Middle Ages in the West. It remains the common practice among lay folk in the East to this day.

Holy Communion has a sociological dimension

Now while the Catholic Church is open to all comers (no prior qualifications, or attainment, or race or other personal characteristics are stipulated) She has a definite purpose and significance. It is simply impossible to belong to Her while not sharing that purpose and affirming that significance. It is for the hierarchy to determine, when necessary, who in fact adequately satisfies these criteria. To this end the Church has adopted a number of creedal statements and oaths of allegiance.

Manifestly, no-one can judge what is in the heart of another. All that the leadership of the Church can insist on is that those who wish to be formally associated with Her, represent Her in the world and speak on Her behalf, must make occasional public profession of faith and acceptance of jurisdiction, as is judged appropriate. Those who refuse to do so when required thereby exclude themselves from Her formal fellowship, though they may be in good faith and so invisibly still attached to Her.

Those who so dissociate themselves from Her jurisdiction necessarily separate themselves from Her commonality, and so from formal association with Her worship and all other details of Her corporate life. This necessarily includes the physical reception of Holy Communion. Communion is not only a transaction between an individual human being and God, but is also an expression of community belonging. The Holy Eucharist is a fellowship meal as well as a propitiatory oblation and worship holocaust. It nourishes and expresses community bonds of fellowship. When an individual receives communion from the community altar, they is assert allegiance to and claim protection from the community. If they do not in fact have such allegiance then their act is a lie and risks being a sacrilege.

Any-one who believes they are right to dissent so far from the consensus of what they recognize as the Official Church that they find themselves excluded from Her worship must also believe that this corporation has itself deviated gravely from the Gospel. They should then feel no compunction in setting themselves up as a better alternative. If they are right, then they can be sure that either they will have in their number those with Apostolic Orders – as is assuredly the case of Old Catholic and Eastern Orthodox jurisdictions – and will be able to obtain the sacraments through the ministry of these persons: or failing that they must conclude that Apostolic Succession is superfluous to the life of the true Christian people – as most Protestant churches have done.

In no case does it make sense to complain that one is deprived of Holy Communion. All that one is being deprived of is sociological association with certain persons with whom one does not really want to be associated with. This kind of complaint generally signifies an internal conflict. The individual in question half believes that they are themselves right and half believes that the Church hierarchy is right. This is a sad torture to endure, but it generally resolves itself one way or the other in a reasonable period of time.

The pros and cons of hierarchy

> I have little respect for hierarchies, and wonder if there is
> any chance that this would be the form God would choose
> to interact with the world and its people.

I don't much like hierarchies, either. However, I simply can't
conceive of any viable alternative.

Jesus explicitly tells those who are first in the Church they
they should conceive of their role as servants not as tyrants.[22]
Sometimes this is a pedagogical role, and sometimes this requires
the use of sanctions. St Paul makes this clear in many places.[23]
Sometimes Christian leadership means "loosing chains", forgiving
sins and opening locks; sometimes it means "binding bonds",
retaining sins and locking doors. Always, authority must be
exercised for what is genuinely perceived to be the objective
benefit of those governed.

Jesus himself appointed twelve intimates to be his "first line
reports". He then appointed seventy others to be "middle
management". The necessities of the human condition required
Him to do this, following the example of Moses, to which I have
already referred.[15]

> A lot of the Church's actions to me seem aimed at hurting
> the honest, and encourage the majority to just pretend to
> go along with things while having no real respect for the
> Church's authority. If the Church only excommunicates
> those with integrity, what does that say to the rest?

I agree that this is an unfortunate practical consequence of much
of the misguided policy of the Church's leadership. On the other
hand, some limits have to be set for what can be approved and
what can be tolerated. Otherwise one is forced to adopt the
"Anglican Model" in which no notion of truth remains.

---

22 Mt 20:25-28.
23 1Cor 4:21; 5:3-5, 12-13; 11:34. 2Cor 7:8-12; 10:8-9.
   1Tim 1:20; 5:20. 2Tim 4:2. Tit 2:15; 3:10-11.

> What right does someone – who has never met me and lives thousands of miles away in a totally different environment – have to make pronouncements as to how I should live my life. My view is: first get to know me, and show me that you are my friend. Then you have some right to question my behaviour.

I agree, except that some behaviours (actions in contexts) are manifestly vicious. One does not need to first become someone's friend in order to condemn their extortion, exploitation of the poor, fraud, pollution of the environment, sexual assault of infants, vilification of the Jews, or adultery. While some details about the circumstances of the actions will be required before judgement can be passed, it is not necessary that a personal relationship be established. Of course, if one seeks to influence behaviour, rather than merely evaluate it as right or wrong, then what you say is correct without qualification. However, that is not the case that you put. You speak of a "right to question" rather than an "effectiveness in influencing."

Jesus is primarily concerned to influence those whom came to Him in good faith. Hence He is called "Friend of Sinners." However, this did not stop Him from condemning in the most certain and extreme terms those in authority whom He judged to be acting in bad faith.

> My contact with the Catholic Church suggests it is more interested in members agreeing to abide by its rules than in what is good for those people.

This is a direct result of the Church having taken on-board Aristotelian metaphysics, anthropology and ethics. It is done in good faith, but is woefully misguided. The top level of the hierarchy generally believes that "its rules" are identical with "what is good for all people."

> In essence it wants to maintain its political, hierarchical power, allowing one person at the top to make a rule for everybody, rather than finding out in love what is best for each individual to do.

Most Catholic bishops honestly believe that the approach which you favour is indistinguishable from moral anarchy. They sincerely believe that it will lead to the loss of all absolute ethical principles and do grave harm both to society at large and to the individuals which constitute it. Personally, I am with you: as long as you agree with me that there do exist objective tests and measures of "what is good" apart from just "immediate gratification", "expedience", "local advantage" and "mutual consent". If this is denied, then the fears of the Vatican are entirely justified.

> The latter could never happen in a hierarchy, unless the person at the top gives up most of their power, focussing on making sure the tier directly below them are "good".

As is often the case, when criticizing something you come up with exactly the answer to your own criticism. Hierarchies don't have to be authoritarian. Each layer could conceive of its role as keeping the layer beneath it from doing harm to those it has authority over. I saw a moving drama at the Edinburgh Fringe in 2002, where a Scottish King asserted that his job was to keep the barons in check, and to act as a champion of the common folk. King Charles the First made a similar point in the final speech he made to his parliamentary executioners.

> One person cannot know everyone in an institution well enough to make informed decisions about how each person should behave.

Agreed. This is one of the reasons for adopting a hierarchical structure. You confuse hierarchy with "top-down command economy." In a healthy hierarchy, information and influence can – and should – pass upwards as well as downwards.

> It is possible that one priest may know the members of his congregation well enough, but even then, it seems unlikely.

Indeed, hence the necessity for the ministry of the deacon and minor orders.

> I think that blanket rules to cover everyone are generally bad. "Teach us how to think, not what to think."

This is authentically "Platonic", in tune with the wisdom of Socrates. However, sometimes it is nice to have a few clues. It is too overwhelming a prospect for most mortals to face the task of figuring everything out for themselves from scratch.

The Cosmological Argument

It is a fundamental expectation of Physics that every thing which one encounters will be *contingent*. Simply put, this means that it always makes sense to ask about any thing, event, process or phenomenon: "Why is this what it is?" or: "How did (or does) this come to be what it is?" or: "What gave (or gives) rise to this?" In other words, the physicist presumes that everything which they experience or observe requires explanation. It is never acceptable to say merely: "This is exactly what it is simply because it is so. It just has to be that way. There is no need to inquire further. You can and must simply accept it for what it is." Physics does not deal in "Just So Stories."[1]

Now any attempt to explain some thing or event by referring it to other things and events is unsatisfactory. First, because such explanations always refer to general laws as well as to particular things, and these laws are themselves facts, with no trace of self evidence or necessity about them; so the question always arises: "Why are these laws what they are?" Second, the other things and events require explaining just as much as does the thing or event which they are supposed to explain.

No extension of this kind of explanation can remove this basic defect and once this is clearly understood, it would seem to follow that the whole Cosmos must itself be contingent. After all, it is entirely constituted of objects and laws which each require explaining.

For a Physicist, the Cosmos certainly requires an explanation. The Physicist wants to have answers to the following questions. How did the Cosmos come to be what in fact is? Why does space-time happen to have the dimensionality which in fact it does have?[2] Why is the Cosmos in the low entropy state which we find it to be in, when this would seem to be so very unlikely? Why is it governed by those laws of Physics by which in actual fact it is governed, rather than by some other set of laws?

---

1   This whole chapter is taken from GOB cap 14.
2   Three space dimensions and one time dimension.

Why do the fundamental constants which feature in these laws have the values which in fact they do have?

Even if the laws of Physics are eventually shown to be necessary (in the sense that if there are to be any such laws, then they must be the very ones that they are) the question "Why are there any laws at all?" will still require an answer. This is a query about being and not-being, not about any particular way of being and, as such, it seems to be unavoidable. One can label the required explanation for the being of all things: "God, the Uncaused Cause, the Ungoverned Governor, the Unmoved Mover, and so on."

The riposte "All you've done is to replace the problem: 'What made the World?' with the problem: 'What caused God?'" is easily answered. The expectation of Physics that "reality is contingent" only relates to that category of being called "things". Things are those beings with which a material observer can interact (directly or indirectly) by an exchange of energy and momentum. With regards to beings other than "things" (if indeed there are such beings) Physics has no expertise or expectations whatsoever.

If God is real, then God is outside space-time, is not part of the Cosmos and does not interact with physical reality in the sense of exchanging energy and momentum with any thing. Although God is the foundation of all physicality, God has no physicality at all. God does not exist in the way that any physical thing exists. God upholds the laws of Physics but is not governed by them. God is "no thing" and these laws simply do not apply to God as such; though they may constrain God's actions in the physical world. We can have no legitimate prior expectations of God, beyond God's reality.

We are therefore free to postulate (being motivated to do so by the pressing need to solve the contingency problem) that God is non-contingent; which means that God is necessary or absolute being. In other words, God is what God is because God is unavoidably so. God (who is "no thing") is real in a manner that no other being is real.

It would therefore seem that:

1. There is a first cause, which can be labelled God.
2. God is extra-cosmic; that is, God is neither a part of the Universe nor identical with the Universe as a whole.
3. God is Necessary Being and the Uncaused Cause.
4. God brings all Cosmic things and events into being via a metaphysical dependence which is entirely different from the physical causation of one event by another.

Some alternatives to Monotheism

There are a three alternatives to this conclusion. They are:

1. **Solipsism:** the entire Cosmos is itself imaginary.
2. **Polytheism:** the basic presumption of Physics is wrong.
3. **Pantheism:** the Cosmos as a whole is not contingent.

Solipsism

The theory that the Cosmos is imaginary and that the only thing which exists is my mind amounts to the idea that I am myself God. Although this position is formally irrefutable, the fact that it entails the idea that I can imagine geniuses such as Plato, daVinci, Bach, Shakespear, Newton, Rembrant, Blake, Maxwell, Einstein, Rachmaninov, Tolstoy, Dali, and Dirac – who are all capable of work which is utterly beyond my own competence – renders it implausible.

Polytheism

Rather than conceiving of one God external to the Cosmos, a number of local deities are postulated. These are sources of being (space-time itself and the physical laws which go with it) and are the uncaused causes of every other thing. It is important to appreciate that Polytheism with one god is not at all the same as Monotheism; as this single god would exist as a thing within the Cosmos and so would certainly violate the laws of Physics.

Polytheism is incoherent. If there was a thing which was necessary then it would of necessity be ubiquitous, because it would be just as true that it was necessary at every place and at every time; so there would have to be an infinity of gods, divinity entirely filling up the cosmos. Now this is either absurd, as entirely at odds with the empirical evidence, or else equivalent to Pantheism or Monotheism – depending on how one envisaged this filling up. Any attempt to avoid this conclusion by conceiving of the gods as non-necessary channels of necessity, can best be understood as a return to Monotheism; with the complication that creation is understood as being mediated by contingent beings – which one might justifiably call angels rather than gods.

The Problem with Pantheism

Pantheism is the hypothesis that the Cosmos is identical with God. This hypothesis only has significance when independent accounts of "Cosmos" and "God" have been given; for without separate accounts of these two terms their identification is trivial.

The Cosmos is the sum total of all material/physical things which exist. More precisely, on the one hand it is constituted of Space-Time and on the other hand of Momentum-Energy.

God is the uncaused first cause, which must be pure act and not have any passivity to, or dependence on, or origin in any other object of thought.

It may seem at first sight that Pantheism is the simplest solution to the classical Cosmological Argument. The idea being that although every individual thing (and even every large collection of things) is contingent, the entirety of all things might not be contingent.

Pantheism, however, does not accord either with experience or physical theory. God is supposed to be good and just; but the Cosmos does not seem so. Nature as revealed by Biology is cruel, violent and wasteful. Human reality is full of suffering and injustice. This is a serious problem for Monotheism, where a clear distinction is made between God and the Cosmos. It is a fatal problem for Pantheism, where the two are identified.

God is eternal and immutable; but the Cosmos is neither.
The "Block Universe" theory[1] implies a kind of eternity and
immutability; but I think not of a kind sufficient to qualify
as divinity. It is certainly not any kind of answer to the problem
of suffering, as all it can say of the brief life of a child born
to a starving mother is that its tragic history is eternally
unanswered, unjustified and unvindicated: as a silent scream
transfixed in amber.

God is complete, self-determined, self-adequate, self-realising
and necessary; but the Cosmos is contingent – this is obvious and
was certainly apparent to classical and scholastic philosophers.
If one says that there is a "spiritual dimension" to the Cosmos
which resolves this indeterminacy, this is exactly equivalent
to opting for Monotheism: as this "spiritual dimension"
is readily identifiable as God. It is impossible to explain
the reality of this spiritual dimension in terms of material
existence – which it transcends, of necessity – whereas
it is simple to explain physical existence as being derived from
such a spiritual reality.

Pantheism is also falsified by the fact that the Universe
is "fine tuned" (in many ways) to be compatible with life.[2]
If there is no rationality apart from the Cosmos itself, then there

---

1 In a Block Universe, time is nothing other than a fourth dimension
   like the three spatial dimensions. Just as one does not think of "left"
   being intrinsically different from "right", but only conventionally so,
   and just as there is no necessity or natural tendency to continually
   relocate one's position further and further to the left; so in a Block
   Universe there is no bias as regards time and no basis on which time
   could be said to flow.

   In a Block Universe, "before" and "after" are interchangeable.
   While there is a sequence of events, there is no means by which
   to fundamentally distinguish "has been" from "will be". Moreover,
   there is no reason why there should be a special moment in time that
   is somehow "now" and hence more real and actual than any other
   moment; any more than there is any special place in space which is
   more real and actual than any other.

2 GOB cap 14.
   P. Davies "The Goldilocks Enigma" (2006)
   See also page 127ff.

can be no explanation for the actual fact that the rationality of the Cosmos is oriented towards life. Apart from the Cosmos there can be no motive or selection criterion for this empirical datum. Hence there is a clear and certain need for either an intelligibility apart from – and transcendent of – the Cosmos, or else for a Multiverse of alternates; but the existence of such a Multiverse would contradict the basic tenet of Pantheism: that the Cosmos is self-adequate and, in effect, divine.

As far as I am aware no serious Physicist contemplates the idea that the Cosmos is self-adequate: this is because Physics has not found any hint of this being the case, rather the contrary! In fact many Cosmologists pursue the Multiverse Theory, as the best (apparently atheistic) explanation for physical existence.

The alternative to Pantheism is Panentheism, which is the orthodox form of Monotheism. This is the theory that God is present within, beneath and beyond every element of the Cosmos, without being identified with the Cosmos. It is indicated by the teaching of Jesus Christ that God knows the number of hairs on our heads,[3] that God is with every sparrow that dies,[4] that charitable works are all done – in the end – to Christ Himself;[5] and the teaching of the fourth evangelist to the effect that the divine logos is the basis of the "nous" (or understanding) of every human being.[6]

The presence of God in physical existent beings (God's imminence) is three-fold. God is present: first, by exact, detailed, precise, exhaustive and intimate knowledge; second, by substantive causality – without God no thing could exist at all: all existence is an energetic[7] participation in God's own essential[7] self-realisation; and third, by benevolent concern.

---

3   Mt 10:30. Lk 12:7.

4   Mt 10:29. Lk 12:6.

5   Mt 25:40.

6   Jn 1:4, 9.

7   The energy-essence distinction is typical of Byzantine rather than Roman theology. The divine essence is "what God is, as being God" whereas the divine energies are "what God does, with regards to the Cosmos."

This imminence is best explained (as a matter of speculation or analogy) as the Cosmos being the imagination of God: God's thinking-through and working-out of all relationships, processes and situations which are possible, given the plethora of excellencies (the ideal forms) that constitute the divine nature. On this account of things, the Cosmos is God's telling and showing of the definitive story of being – the epitome of all novels and plays – in which we are characters and actors.

This account reconciles God's transcendence (otherness, immateriality, imperturbability, non-contingency) with God's imminence (presence, involvement, accessibility, relevance) without compromising either. God's nature as God (the divine essence[7]) is unknowable and entirely beyond our experience – as also, it would seem, is the nature of our own consciousness.[8]

_____

8 UPSY

The Argument from Design [1]

Given that I exist, I must of necessity do so in a Cosmos which is suitable for my existence. This observation is called the Weak Anthropic Principle. It follows from this truism that I must observe that the Cosmos is suitable for my survival. Those aspects of cosmic order which appear tuned to allow for our specific kind of life require no additional rationale. Values for the constants of Physics incompatible with the formation of carbon based macro-molecules would only rule out our own type of life, not life in general. Even if the laws of Physics were very different, then although I would not exist, some other form of life might well do so and be asking questions like "why is the Cosmos just right for me?" in my stead.

However, I shall next argue that if any of the laws of Physics were to be changed even slightly, then no life of **any** kind could have come into being. This contention is called the Strong Anthropic Principle. If it is true it is indisputably queer that the Cosmos is suitable for my existence in such a singular manner, and it would seem that the Universe had to be carefully engineered in order to allow for the emergence of life. Professor Paul Miller puts the case as follows:

> Although the specifics of carbon Chemistry… may not be necessary for life… a living being must contain organized complexity, or information… [which] requires… a local decrease in entropy.
>
> Entropy is… the disorder in a system, and… entropy always increases… cups fall and shatter, they do not coalesce and jump back onto their saucers. More importantly, without sustenance and breath, bodies die and decay, while corpses do not come back to life.

---

1   This whole chapter is taken from GOB cap 14.

A living being with the ability to ask the question "why am I here?" must contain an incredible amount of order to be able to frame such a deep, information filled thought, whatever kind of Chemistry or Physics underlies the being.

So the question is, "what kinds of Universe could allow such order to arise?" If the answer is "just about any" then we should not be so surprised about our Universe – the right, well suited type of order would arise to fit the environment in any Universe. However, if the answer is "almost none", then we do need to question why the Universe is so special.[2]

Of course, if there are an infinite number of Universes, each with its own distinctive Physics, then there is nothing to explain. No matter how unusual it is for a Universe to be "life friendly", those few which are so will give rise to life, and whenever life achieves consciousness it will start writing books like this one.

This possibility is known as the Multiverse Hypothesis. It conflicts with the hope of many theoreticians that only one Physics is coherent. If its laws featured no arbitrary parameters, then everything would be explained – except for the fundamental question: "Why is there anything at all?" It would, however, be truly remarkable if the only possible set of laws and fundamental constants is exactly the one which we know gives rise to life in such a precarious manner.[3]

On the Multiverse account of reality, one avoids invoking an infinite Creator as the designer of the Cosmos at the expense of postulating an infinite (or extremely large) set of worlds.[4]

---

2 P. Miller "The Anthropic Principle"
3 This would mean that logic itself necessitates life. The prologue of John's Gospel, [Jn 1:1-4] with its statement that the Logos is both the principle of creation and the basis of life can be construed as presenting exactly this doctrine.
4 Arguably, this set constitutes "the mind of God" under another name.

It is, however, possible to make the Multiverse hypothesis more palatable, as Miller describes:

> Many cosmologists are attempting to find what explanation they can within Science, in preference to invoking a Creator... the ripples left on the cosmic background radiation... provide strong evidence for a period of... exponential expansion... in the first 10-33 seconds of the Universe's existence. If such an era existed... There could be a plethora of... sub-Universes, that are completely unobservable to us... it is not so surprising that one of a multitude of sub-Universes happens to have the right conditions for life.

As someone suspicious of the application of probability theory to reality, I cannot resist pointing out that this argument is all about how likely it is that the Cosmos is exactly how it is. Given that the Cosmos is in fact what it is; we know the probability (in one sense of the word) that it is so; namely unity. Only if one can legitimately conceive of a set of equally likely alternatives (and this necessitates knowledge of a symmetry of some unknown system which is supposed to underlie all possible Universes) can one start to ask questions such as: "What proportion of all possible Universes are compatible with life?"

String theory is typically put forward to serve as the underlying system. This unsubstantiated theory has the property of being compatible with a large number of highly diverse types of space-time. Hence, if every possible variant of space-time is arbitrarily taken to have the same basic probability and to have somehow occurred, then "it is not so surprising that one of a multitude of sub-Universes happens to have the right conditions for life." However, what is being done here is to explain a finitely surprising particular (that is, the existence of sentient life) in terms of an infinity of unsurprising particulars. It is not at all clear to me that this is a worthwhile enterprise.

Miller continues:

It is well known that all life on Earth (barring the strange
sulphurous life arising around deep-sea volcanic vents)
is ultimately dependent on the inflowing energy from
the sun. The sun is an average star, and, like all stars,
can provide the power for life, by providing vast amounts
of energy (as heat and light) at very low entropy (from
a small region much hotter than the rest of the Universe).

Hot spots, such as stars, are necessary to allow any
form of organized complexity to arise. Living things must
all take in low entropy (hot or organized) energy and
release it at high entropy (useless waste heat) in order
to increase or at least maintain their internal information.
The "hot spots" which allow any living being to survive,
must also be there for it to evolve, so must remain stable
over a large period of time, compared to typical physical
processes in the life cycle of the being.

Now, in our Universe there is a specific resonance
in the nuclear reaction process, which enables stars
to burn at all, and endure for the billions of years that
have been necessary for life to develop. In a Universe
almost the same as ours, but perhaps with a slightly
different electron mass, the resonance would not occur,
stars would not shine, and the Universe would be dark,
dead and dull.[5]

There is a multitude of similarly finely tuned
properties of our Universe... The delicate balance
between the original expansion of the Universe and the
gravitational attraction, which tends to pull everything
back together, ensures that the explosive debris from one
star can arrive in the vicinity of another star which forms
separately. All life on Earth is made from atoms of debris
from the first star, and relies on heat and light from the

---

5   Sir. Fred Hoyle was the astrophysicist who discovered this fact.
    He was an atheist at the time, but subsequently became a convinced
    Theist.

second star, namely our sun. In a gravitationally stronger Universe, the first star would swallow the second, while in a… more spread-out Universe, the debris would never reach another star.

This is a telling argument. Darwinism can't help here. Even if the laws of Physics could mutate, it is difficult to see how natural selection could operate. Of course, it might just be that the Cosmos is a self-consistent solution. The idea being that the Cosmos was created (or the laws of Physics at least massaged) by gods who evolve within the Cosmos and then travel back to the beginning of time to ensure that the Cosmos starts off just right. Miller expresses a related idea, more prosaically:

A similarly untestable possibility put forth by scientific skeptics is that the Universe is really infinite in time, and just bounces in and out of big crunches[6] and big bangs. There is supposedly a new set of laws of Physics each time round (though, this is rather implausible in my view, as the new mashed-up fundamental laws must always lead to another bouncing Universe, without being specifically tuned!)

Miller concludes as follows:

While scientific skeptics deny the Strong Anthropic Principle, many theologians and religious scientists embrace it, as it points to a Creator who stimulates life and enables us to flourish. The uncovering of such a fertile Universe, which is so clearly conducive to beauty, encourages process theologians, as it appears that the Universe follows a very thin line between rigid order and incoherent chaos. Other religious thinkers remain wary of the whole argument, and… are loathe to incorporate any scientific evidence, which may be later

---

6   More recent observations indicate that the expansion of the Cosmos is accelerating rather than slowing down, so it will never reverse and the Cosmos will not end in a "Big Crunch".

reinterpreted, in their vision of God. As the "many Universe" theories are not completely outside the realms of falsifiable evidence, it is perhaps right to be patient before hailing the fine-tuning as proof of God. Nevertheless, I for one do not cease to be amazed by the transcendent beauty inherent within the Laws of Nature. These will always speak to me of the nature of God.

The Ontological Argument[1]

Even the fool is convinced that something exists in the understanding, at least, than which nothing greater can be conceived. For when he hears of this, he understands it, and whatever is understood exists in the understanding; and assuredly that "than which nothing greater can be conceived" cannot exist in the understanding alone. For suppose it exists in the understanding alone; then it can be conceived to exist in reality, which is greater. Therefore, if that "than which nothing greater can be conceived" exists in the understanding alone, the very being "than which nothing greater can be conceived" is one than which a greater can be conceived; but obviously this is impossible. Hence, there is no doubt that there exists a being "than which nothing greater can be conceived" and it exists both in the understanding and in reality. [Anselm, Archbishop of Canterbury[2]]

The Ontological Argument uses the idea of perfection, greatness or superiority to show that the Greatest Conceivable Being is necessarily real. It can be parodied as follows: "Because it is possible to conceive of 'the best possible thing' and it is better to be real than not, then the best possible thing must be real." In this presentation the Ontological Argument is clearly flawed, because at best it only proves that one must *conceive* of the best possible thing as being real – which is no great surprise.

Similarly, it is possible to imagine "the Best Tooth-pick", which would not be the best if it did not exist – therefore it must be *imagined* as existing! However, to infer that this means that the Best Possible Toothpick actually exists is faulty logic. All we have done is show that the "Best Possible Toothpick" must be *imagined* as existing, not that it must actually do so.

---

1   This whole chapter is taken from GOB cap 14.
2   1033AD–1109AD.

Even if it is granted that a supremely perfect being brings existence with him because of his very title, it still doesn't follow that the existence in question is anything actual in the real world, all that follows is that the concept of existence is inseparably linked to the concept of a supreme being. So you can't infer that the existence of God is something actual (unless you help yourself to the premise that the supreme being actually exists, in which case he will actually contain all perfections, including the perfection of real existence!)
[R. Descartes "Objections and Replies" (1641)]

The fact that we can frame a concept which can only be coherently conceived as corresponding to an existent being, does not mean that this being actually exists.[3] However, as we shall see, the Ontological Argument has much greater force than this when properly presented. Nevertheless,

If you attend carefully to this difference between the idea of God and every other idea, you'll undoubtedly see that, even though our understanding of other things always involves thinking of them as if they existed, it doesn't follow that they do exist but only that they could. Our understanding doesn't show us that actual existence must be conjoined with their other properties, but from our understanding that actual existence is conjoined, necessarily and always with God's other attributes, it certainly does follow that God exists.
[R. Descartes "Objections and Replies" (1641)]

---

3   Apart from "Lovatt's Lemma", see page 11.

Something is not quite right

Now, in the Ontological Argument, the phrase "Greatest Conceivable Being" can be replaced everywhere by "Greatest Conceivable Tooth-pick" (or GCT) without changing the structure of the syllogism. The extravagant conclusion follows that the GCT is real. Recognising this difficulty, skeptics generally assert that what I have designated as the minor premise is flawed.

> The most definitive refutations of the Ontological Argument are usually attributed to the philosophers David Hume and Immanuel Kant. Kant identified the trick card up Anselm's sleeve as his slippery assumption that existence is more perfect than non-existence. The American philosopher Norman Malcolm put it like this: "The doctrine that existence is a perfection is remarkably queer. It makes sense and is true to say that my future house will be a better one if it is insulated than if it is not insulated; but what could it mean to say that it will be a better house if it exists than if it does not?"[4]
> [R. Dawkin "The God Delusion" (2006)]

Kant believed that the flaw in the argument is that it treats existence as a first-order predicate; that is, a descriptor which adds something to the constitution of an entity. On the contrary, he asserted that a thing's nature is not enhanced by it existing; and that whether a thing exists or not is incidental to its perfection.

> Being is evidently not a real predicate, that is, a conception of something which is added to the conception of some other thing. It is merely the positing of a thing, or of certain determinations in it... The proposition "God is omnipotent" contains two conceptions, which have a certain object or content; the word "is" is no additional predicate – it merely

---

4   N. Malcolm "Anselm's Ontological Argument" (1960)

indicates the relation of the predicate to the subject. Now, if I take the subject (God) with all its predicates (omnipotence being one), and say "God is" or "There is a God" I add no new predicate to the conception of God, I merely posit or affirm the existence of the subject with all its predicates – I posit the object in relation to my conception. The content of both is the same; and there is no addition made to the conception (which expresses merely the possibility of the object) by my cogitating the object – in the expression "it is" – as absolutely given or existing. Thus the real contains no more than the possible.

[I. Kant "Critique of Pure Reason" IV (1791)]

From this it follows that a GCB conceived of as imaginary is no less than a GCB conceived of as real.

"God is omnipotent" – that is a necessary judgement. His omnipotence cannot be denied, if the existence of a Deity is posited... But when you say "God does not exist" neither omnipotence nor any other predicate is affirmed; they must all disappear with the subject, and in this judgement there cannot exist the least self-contradiction... I find myself unable to form the slightest conception of a thing which when annihilated in thought with all its predicates, leaves behind a contradiction; and contradiction is the only criterion of impossibility in the sphere of pure a priori conceptions.

[I. Kant "Critique of Pure Reason" IV (1791)]

I do not believe that Hume, Kant and Malcolm are correct. I think that it is pretty obvious that a real house is much to be preferred over an imaginary one. After all, what does "better" mean? It means something along the lines of: "provides greater advantage to its possessor in regard to those matters in which it might be expected to be advantageous," or else: "serves its purpose more adequately."

Now a house existing only as a set of plans provides no advantage – as a house – to its possessor whatsoever. A house that is real (even if it is far from the ideal house) is indefinitely better (that is, more effective) than one which exists only in concept or, in other words, is imaginary. However, the plans for a mansion (together with funds adequate to construct it) might be preferable to an actually existing log cabin.

This is indicative of the fact that it is impossible to establish a unique metric for "better" when more than a single criterion (such as total floor area, resilience to earthquake damage, level of thermal insulation) is involved. Which is better: a gloriously beautiful palace made of glass, which is impossible to keep warm and which would collapse as a result of the slightest earth-tremor; or a small but cosy cottage with thick stone walls and a thatched roof supported on strong oak beams? In truth, it is impossible to identify one thing as greater than another thing unless the former excels (or at least equals) the latter in every regard.

In connexion with God, the matter is simple. An imaginary "God" is of no utility whatsoever to its own unreality, and of little utility to whatever being happened to conceive of it. It is indefinitely better for God that God is real, and it is pretty obvious that this is better for humanity too – given the advantage that might be hoped to accrue from an association with the real God.

The absurdity of necessary existence

Hume attacks the Ontological Argument in a second way. He asserts that as anything which can be conceived of as existing can just as well be conceived of as not existing, the very idea of "the necessary existent being" is absurd.

> I shall begin with observing, that there is an evident absurdity in pretending to demonstrate a matter of fact, or to prove it by any arguments a priori. Nothing is demonstrable unless the contrary implies a contradiction. Whatever we conceive as existent, we can also conceive as non-existent. There is no being, therefore, whose non-existence implies a contradiction. Consequently there is no being, whose existence is demonstrable.

I propose this argument as entirely decisive, and am willing to rest the whole controversy upon it. It is pretended, that the deity is a necessarily existent being, and this necessity of His existence is attempted to be explained by asserting, that, if we knew His whole essence or nature, we should perceive it to be as impossible for Him not to exist as for twice two not to be four. But it is evident, that this can never happen, while our faculties remain the same as at present... The words, therefore, "necessary existence" have no meaning; or which is the same thing, none that is consistent. [D. Hume "Dialogues Concerning Natural Religion" (1779)]

In my view, Hume is largely correct in the assertions he makes here; but is nevertheless mistaken in the conclusion which he draws.

First, I agree that any attempt to argue the reality of God out of nothing is doomed to failure. How could it possibly be valid to establish such a momentous result without reference to anything at all? However, the Ontological Argument in fact rests on a number of background premises, many of which are in principle disputable. They might be enumerated as follows: (1) Thought can and ought to be rational and the rules of classical logic are a good representation of rationality. (2) It is correct to speak of beings and it is correct to make a distinction between "real" and "imaginary" beings. (3) It is correct to speak of "value" and of "more" and "less". (4) It is possible, in principle, to attribute relative value to beings according to various criteria. (5) It is better for a being to be real than to be imaginary, every other aspect of its constitution being unchanged.

Now, denying any of these basic premises has a much wider impact on one's world-view than making one an Atheist rather than a Theist. It is therefore not true that the Ontological Argument produces God out of a hat, or defines God into existence. Rather, what it shows is that it not possible to be a rational Objective Realist without being a Theist too.

In other words, the Ontological Argument shows that the structure of the Cosmos as we experience and understand it is indicative of it being derivative of Absolute Being.

Second. I agree that nothing is demonstrated conclusively unless its converse is shown to be absurd. However, this is exactly what the Ontological Argument claims to do.

Third, I agree that any thing which exists might just as well not do so. However, the Ontological Argument does not deal with physical existence but rather with reality; and it is not at all clear that every being which is real might not be so. *This is in fact exactly the point at issue.* To simply presume that all of reality is contingent is to fatally prejudice the question.

Finally, I concede that it is ludicrous to suggest that the human mind could comprehend the Divine Nature, should there be such. However, it turns out that it is not necessary to do so in order to understand how it is that God is necessary being.

The incompatibility objection

It can be argued that the GCB is a contradiction in terms as some perfections are incompatible, not just incommensurate. Hence, whereas it is possible for a being to be both perfectly square and perfectly circular if its reality is at least three-dimensional;[5] it is not possible for a judge to be both perfectly just and perfectly merciful. This is, supposedly, because justice amounts to "giving to each subject exactly what they deserve" and mercy amounts to being more generous than this, at least in some cases. Hence justice and mercy are in conflict and it is impossible to be perfectly just and perfectly merciful. Multiplying dimensions simply doesn't help here.

To this objection I reply by questioning its basic assumption that any perfections can be absolutely contradictory. In particular, I reject the definitions of mercy and justice that the example entails. So far as God is concerned, no created being actually deserves anything of its own right; so all of God's actions towards

---

5   This is a cylinder with a length equal to its diameter.

creatures are essentially those of mercy[6] not justice. However, it is only proportionate, right and proper that God does act towards creatures with mercy; for else they could not exist and the very act of creation would be made into an absurdity. So, in God justice and mercy do not conflict but are aspects of the same reality.

Moreover, it is also just of God to be merciful to the sinner in view of the fact that God foresees that in the future they will be a saint, if only God is presently merciful. Arguably, the same is true in the human context also. It is just to be merciful; where mercy means giving a culprit a chance to repent and change their ways. It is merciful to be just; where justice means imposing a penalty which is crafted to bring about penitence and reformation in the heart of the wrongdoer.

I maintain that any other supposed examples of incompatible perfections could be dealt with either by postulating a sufficient dimensionality for God or else by elucidating the true nature of the perfections involved and in doing so establishing that their apparent incompatibility is illusory.

The real subtlety

The real subtlety with the Ontological Argument – the feature that invalidates the extravagant conclusion that "the Greatest Conceivable Triangle" or "the Greatest Conceivable Toothpick exists" – is quite different from what Hume, Kant and Malcolm envisage. It is that in conceiving of either of these two GCTs as existing one is forced to derogate from its perfection.

---

6   The word mercy does not simply mean "letting someone off a punishment which they deserve as a result of misbehaviour". It also means kindness, generosity and benevolence. The "Good Samaritan" was, in this sense, merciful to the man who had been set upon by thieves and left for dead when he came to his aid. [Lk 10:37] When the Eastern Liturgies cry out over and over "Lord, have mercy!" they are not asking for forgiveness, but rather for divine assistance.

Adding *existence* (as opposed to *reality*) to the imaginary Perfect Triangle does not obviously make it "greater", and so one cannot say that the value of the imaginary Perfect Triangle is definitely less than the value of its existent analogue. This is because, while an existing triangle might well be rightly evaluated as greater than a purely imaginary one – in terms of "usefulness", say – so far as its existence goes; any existing triangle is not going to be so perfectly formed a triangle as is the imaginary Perfect Triangle. The existent triangle's vertices will be blunt, not perfect points, and its sides will not be absolutely straight and uniformly – let alone infinitesimally – narrow. This is necessarily true (not incidentally) because the existent triangle will be made either of atoms, or else beams of light perhaps, and mass-energy is always quantal – and approximate in other ways.

Similarly, no physical toothpick could be perfectly sharp, or perfectly rigid, or perfectly resistant to corrosion. Hence when one tries to compare the imaginary GCT with its best possible material realisation, one cannot unequivocally say which is "greater"; for though any physical toothpick has indefinitely greater practical utility, the ideal toothpick is in every theoretical way indefinitely better. Hence one cannot conclude that the GCT conceived of as imaginary is not in fact the GCT, and so one cannot infer that the GCT necessarily exists.

A similar argument will apply to any other "Greatest Conceivable Thing". The granular and quantum-mechanical nature of matter will always prevent its exact physical realization. Hence, there is always at least one "extrinsic circumstance" which necessarily prevents us conceiving of any "Greatest Conceivable Thing" as actually existing. This circumstance is simply "materiality" or "existence" itself; which limitation happily prevents the Ontological Argument from generating a multitude of spurious "Greatest Conceivable Things".

The only existence that is at issue here is necessary existence, which gives the thing that has it the power to create itself or to keep itself in existence, and when

I examine the idea of a body[7] I perceive that no body has such a power as that. From this I infer that necessary existence doesn't belong to the nature of a body – however perfect – any more than being without lowlands belongs to the nature of highlands[8] or having angles summing to more than 180 degrees belongs to the nature of a triangle![9] [R. Descartes "Objections and Replies" (1641)]

However, this circumstance fails to apply as soon as one abstracts one's thought beyond material things to consider beings in general which do not obviously have to be part of the physical contingent order. Hence, the "flaw" that we have identified in the Ontological Argument does not hinder its application to the GCB, which is not supposed to *physically exist*, but rather to *be real*.

Now let us turn from body and consider the idea of a thing[10] – whatever it turns out to be – that has all the perfections that can exist together. Is existence one of these perfections? We will be in some doubt about this at first, because our finite mind is accustomed to thinking of these perfections only separately, so that it may not immediately notice the necessity of their being joined together. But if we address ourselves attentively to the questions "Does existence belong to a supremely powerful being?" and – if it does – "What sort of existence is it?" we'll be able to perceive clearly and distinctly the following facts.

---

7   The word "body" is here used in the way that I use the word "thing".
8   Descartes seems to mean that a highland region might contain some lowlands without ceasing to be a highland region: no existent thing has to be entirely perfect, let alone self-existent.
9   Descartes takes this to be absurd – though, of course, it is not; if the triangle is drawn on the surface of a sphere.
10 In this translation, Descartes uses "thing" in the way that I use "being". Note that the rest of this extract employs the word "being".

(1) Possible existence, at the very least, belongs to such a being, just as it belongs to everything else of which we have a distinct idea, even if it's an idea put together through a fiction of the intellect.[11]

(2) When we attend to the immense power of this supremely powerful being we shan't be able to think of its existence as possible without also recognising that the being can exist by its own power, from which we'll infer that it really does exists and has existed from eternity.[12] [R. Descartes "Objections and Replies" (1641)]

---

[11] Because the GCB is conceivable, by definition, it is certain that the GCB involves no absurdity or self-contradiction. Hence it is also certain that the GCB might be real: there is nothing about the GCB in itself which precludes it from being real.

[12] The final step in Descartes' argument is mistaken, as it is presented here. The fact that some particular being, if real, would be capable of subsisting of itself does not entail that this being is in fact real and does self-subsist; but only that if it were real, it would not be dependent for its subsistence on any extrinsic circumstance. What is needed to close the gap is "Lovatt's Lemma".

Nyxosrates: a Platonic dialogue

Good day, Nyxosrates; how are things with you?

Hello, Theophilus, I am well enough. Nothing really changes, you know.

How is that, my friend?

Well, it seems to me that the past is an ever present power, and I find it difficult to think that the future will be different.

I know that you've had difficult times, Nyx, and you know that I sympathise. If there is anything I can do to help, just ask and I'll try my best to do what's right.

But what is "right", Theo? It seems to me that there is no "right" – just a surfeit of "wrong". All I see in this world is fakery, lies and suffering: friends who only truly care about their own needs and a Cosmos that is more like a torture chamber than the fertile womb and nurturing breasts of a loving Mother. It seems to me that all I have is my will, and even that is bound fast about by ropes which hold me back and frustrate my flight.

What ropes are those, Nyx? It seems to me that you are as free as any man; and being more reflective than most you have a greater grasp of truth than many a one I know!

The ropes of my experience and of my unwanted nature, Theo. What has happened in the past has taught me to expect nothing better from the future. I think that the world which has been dangerous in every regard up to now will continue to be so in days to come. As the regularity of the seasons establishes precedent for future harvests, so I have no doubt that the horrors of history (both my own and that of humanity at large) will be reproduced time and time again in the future. If my nature was different from what it is, I might fly away from all the turmoil and deceit; but as it is I am trapped in this body of flesh, with its frailties, dependencies and annoying limitations.

I know that you have come through a lot, my friend; and have learned distrust and fear; but you are still alive and that itself should be a reason for hope! As you have survived past travail, so you may expect to survive what else may come your way. You have proved your resilience and shown your courage. Moreover your life is itself a spark of pure potency. There is no telling what the sacred flame which flickers in your heart may ignite, and what beacon-blaze may burn as a result of your creative will, and as a testimony to your vision. There is beauty both in this world and in your heart, and there is always the possibility of joy.

Oh Theo, Theo: you are so naïve! This world is a poor sham of what might be. In my heart I know that there could be a much better place: where there's no pain and all are safe and sound; as chicks gathered gently beneath the wings of the mother hen. Moreover, in that Best of Worlds there would be no disharmony between aspiration and the outcome of attaining ones desire. In this life it is all too common for what is pleasant, pleasurable or attractive in some other way to have a sharp thorn, or bitter after-taste, or else to be close followed by a head-splitting ache.

Well that's a sorry view of things, Nyxos. I'll not spend time pointing out that things are not all bad; for I'm sure that you know as well as I that there are good things hereabouts which give relief from the darkness of which you are so keenly conscious. I will, however, remind you that desirable things often seem only to come with bad side effects – as if one was being punished for desiring what is beautiful or pleasant – because one can have too much of a good thing, and because it is possible to get distracted from what is good in the long-term by what offers immediate gratification.

Hence, oxygen, water, salt and glucose are all good for you; but it is possible to be killed by a surfeit of any of these. Similarly, medicines are generally poisonous if an over-dose is taken. Things are good when used or appropriated or exercised in proportion to the actual need which exists. The fact that it is good to have a trace quantity of copper in ones diet does not mean that any more than that very small amount is better! In fact copper is a very poisonous element. Too much exercise will cripple an athlete. Too much revision will fatigue a student and make them fail their examination. Too much sympathy will make a victim self-indulgent and subvert their will to overcome their afflictions.

Playing with your children is an excellent thing. Perhaps it is impossible to do this to excess; but even so, doing this when one ought to be working would be wrong, and liable to result in poverty. Worship and prayer are also excellent; but, again, devoting oneself to these activities to the extent that one neglected to eat would result in ones death. Moreover, one has obligations to ones fellows and it is wrong to neglect these on the pretext of religious practice. Always, what matters is balance and harmony: each aspect of ones life being coordinated with every other and in proportion with the actual needs and capabilities of ones constitutional make-up.

Moreover some things exist which are alluring, but of no true value. Various psycho-active chemicals come into this category, and also certain addictive activities. These all delude their victims into thinking that they are in fact beneficial, by simply being pleasurable or attractive, when in fact they are only harmful – or at best an obsessive distraction from other things which are necessary for a healthy and happy life. These things are not placed in the world in order to tempt or torture us. They exist of unfortunate necessity: as substances and behaviours which have some commonality or similarity with good things, while not being those good things; and so they fool our appetites and instincts into mistaking them for what is wholesome.

Wisdom allows us to distinguish what seems to be good from what is actually good; and these distractions have no hold on the wise person, because they are seen for the empty shams that they are are in fact.

That may all be so, Theo; but it still seems to me that this world is at best a mess; and either we are mere futile accidents, or else the pathetic playthings of some sadist's sport.

My dear Nyxos, it seems to me you are making one basic mistake, and it is this which causes your dismay. This mistake is the conviction (which on a superficial view I admit seems right) that there is something very wrong with this world which could easily not be so; and that the discrepancy between the evil-that-is and the good-that-might-be is a sign, sure and definite, of basic wrong.

    If this belief were to be refuted, then your case would fail: for if the tragedies of this world were shown to be both necessary and also to contribute (in some hidden way) to an outstanding good, then they would have no power to fright us to the depths of our soul; but only to sadden us a while: as things which trouble for a time, then pass, and finally are gone for good.

I suppose you are right, my friend; but it seems to me your case is most implausible. What good can come from all the conceits of this foul world: from plague and pestilence; from hurricane and tidal-wave; from meteorite and earthquake? The wrongs of human will may be excused by in terms of autonomy, perhaps; but why would One with power sufficient to still the storm and quiet the quaking ground stand by and let innocent children die?

I do not rest my case on any claim that good comes from such bad things, dear heart; though on occasion this is so – or so it seems at least. Moreover, I do not offer any definite proof that things must be exactly as they are: for I have some suspicion (based on subtle argument of necessity) that this world is no more, nor less, than existent possibility; and so may be one of many parallel physical realities. Rather, my case is set on two contentions which cast your gruesome certainty into grave doubt.

Well then, Theo, let's hear your case. How can it be that the manifest evil in this world is not proof positive of either life's essential futility or else that the world's Creator is malign?

My first point, Nyxos, is this: how can you be so sure that the world which you imagine – where all is fair, and right prevails in every particular – is possible in principle? There is a difference, after all, between what may be contrived as fantasy and what is conceivable as potential fact.

Fantasy does not demand that things make sense, or hold together in one great scheme of law and ordered form. In lands of make-believe exceptions abound: wherever forms which are incommensurate, and ideas which have no common ground, rub up against each other, with no single law to reconcile them.

The criterion of conceivability is much more strict than this! For any thing to really exist it must make sense (that is, be "coherent" or "self-compatible") at every level and in every way, down to the finest of details.

It is no more good enough to say: "There could be a world without (or with much less) suffering in it," than to say: "There could be a means for a solid material object to travel faster than the speed of light," or that: "There could be life after death." All of these statements are grammatically sound and seem meaningful enough; but that is not strong enough evidence to prove them true. Perhaps there is a non-obvious reason that the assertion of one or more of these "coulds" is in fact mistaken.

We know for sure that the world we live in is actually conceivable; simply because it does in fact exist. We know (or at least believe, with what seems good cause) that the very existence of this world is based on Universal Physical Law; and that whenever there is some disjuncture of form (as between crystals of ice which grow from different centres on the surface of a pond and then fuse at "grain boundaries"; or between tectonic plates; or across a shock-wave, where pressure changes abruptly; or at the terminus of the rattling dance of a silver ball in a wheel of chance) it is mediated by some transition, however brief, of continuity; and never involves any contradiction of being: where something both "is" and "is not".

The fact that you can imagine a "perfect world of peace and joy" does not mean that in fact it is conceivable, and therefore might well exist. It may be that no such utopia is possible, and until you have established its possible existence beyond the realms of fantasy it has no bearing on the case at hand. Pure speculation cannot be the ground of worthy doubt, and even less of certainty. This is an example of "blind faith" motivated by raw emotion rather than reason or evidence.

Moreover, what is certain is this: any world capable of supporting life is pretty much bound to be subject to regular disaster. This is an issue of mathematics, and not any kind of speculation. The reason is as follows. Life is continuity in flux,[1] and at the most basic level this can only come to be as a result of "non-linearity". The basic law of life is that in certain cases "non-linearity" can compensate for "dissipation": the universal tendency to decay; and that when it does a "soliton" results: a constant form arising from out of a flow – which flow itself supports that form's stability and evacuates its entropy.

Now any system which is non-linear is subject to another characteristic: that of unpredictability. Although it may for an extended while behave in some quasi-constant way (being subject to a "strange attractor") yet this is not all that's to be said; and it is certain that – without warning – this quasi-stability will "glitch" and some unexpected deviance or "catastrophe" occur. This is the basic cause of earthquakes, lightning strikes, tsunamis and disease epidemics. Hence the one actuality (namely: "non-linearity") lies at the root of both "life" and "disasters", and it is impossible to have the one without the other; unless some external agency should intervene at the slightest sign that anything is amiss and so pinch out every catastrophe in the bud.

Hold on, Theo, perhaps you have a point; and yet this train of thought seems to be a problem for you too. If any world that features life must also feature woe and death, then how can you believe in a future world – whether it be "Heaven" or a "Resurrection Home" – that's free from pain? It seems that your argument must make such a place an impossibility; and if that's so, there is no mitigation of our woe, for what you're arguing amounts to this: "Life implies death, get used to it!"

---

1   GOB cap 4.

This pertains to my second point, Nyxos, which is the purpose of this world, and how it might differ from that of the next. Clearly, if it is the case that non-linearity is necessary for life, and that non-linearity also necessitates disasters, then it would seem to follow that Heaven or the "Resurrection Home" promised in the Old and New Testaments of the Bible is an impossibility; and conversely, if they are possible (in spite of my argument that such a place or state is impossible) then your conclusion seems to follow. However, there is a further element that I have mentioned in passing and which we must now consider in detail. This element is "divine intervention" or "actual grace".

The one thing that would make the existence of living beings compatible with an absence of catastrophe is a continual monitoring and correction of the world; so as to ensure that everything that might otherwise "go wrong" is stopped from doing so by extrinsic intervention. God is entirely capable of doing this (being both omniscient and omnipotent) and we must assume that this is roughly what makes Heaven and the "Resurrection Home" possible.

This doesn't change anything, Theo! Can't you see that? If God is capable of breaking the natural link between the non-linearity, which is needful for life to exist, and catastrophe, then why doesn't God do so for us here and now in this world? Why does God forebear to act now and only promise to do so in some indefinite future state of affairs? Your words change nothing at all. Either God chooses to stand by and ignore our suffering, refusing to intervene to ameliorate it; or else God elects to be entertained by it. God is either callous and indifferent, or a sadistic monster, or else has no reality whatsoever!

I understand why you say this, Nyxos. The only answer possible is that God has a sufficient and just reason for not intervening as you think God ought to. It therefore behoves us to inquire as to what this might be. It turns out that there is an obvious explanation, and that this explanation is corroborated by the explicit testimony of both the Old and New Testaments.

I can't see how anything could justify God simply standing by and allowing all the suffering that humanity routinely experiences, Theo. Moreover, it seems to me that it is degrading to attempt to defend God's involvement in that suffering. It is simply monstrous!

Yes, I know how you feel; but the alternative to exonerating God is to have it that God is either worthless to us, or is our sworn enemy, or else is a figment of our wishful thinking. All of those possibilities have unpleasant implications one way or another; but let's not explore those implications for now. Instead allow me to stick with my task and see whether I can propose a defence that will exonerate God of indifference, irresponsibility and cruelty. If I can do this, then it will not be monstrous at all; for I will have shown that God is in fact innocent, and that it is we who are wrong to accuse God of negligence or malice.

I don't like this one bit, Theo; but I suppose that I have to let you try. After all, I must admit that it would be a good result – one that I would be pleased with, and find comforting – if you managed to vindicate God and show that God is benevolent and kind rather than wicked and vicious.

God's obvious defence, Nyxos, is that this world serves as a growth and learning experience for humanity as to the nature of good and evil, so that we can discover for ourselves (rather than by magisterial instruction) which attitudes and dispositions, habits and practices are wholesome: promoting and underpinning well-being, enabling the individual and community to live long and prosper and so to be happy; and which others are perverse: frustrating or undermining life.

You see, for us to understand what is virtuous and what is vicious there have to be outcomes which follow from our actions in accord with comprehensible law. If this was not so there would be no meaning to "virtue" or "right" or "correct". This is because what happened to us and our families, friends and communities would not depend in any definite way on our character, outlook, dispositions, customs and habits; hence no act could be construed as righteous or sinful, as it could not be causally connected to any outcome – or even to a tendency to produce certain kinds of outcome.

Now for there to be any kind of existence there must be a rationale or "Logos" for that existence: a basic framework, under-standing or foundation of law that enables it to function. This certainly seems to be true of the world in which we live, and it is the business of physicists to elucidate this "Logos" or "Theory" ever more clearly. Hence the foundational requirement of ethics "for actions to have intrinsic or natural consequences" is pretty much bound to be met by any conceivable Cosmos, and is definitely met by the one in which we actually live.

The problem with this is that the consequences of certain actions (or inactions!) can sometimes be disproportionate to those actions. If a child ignorantly drinks a small quantity of bleach, their oesophagus can be entirely ruined. If a paraffin lamp is accidentally knocked over, a bystander may suffer terrible burns. If a man kisses his friend's forehead while that friend lies near to death in hospital, he can be accused of being a sexual predator and his relationship with his friend be destroyed. If a person takes a holiday at a Burmese beech resort, they can be drowned in a tsunami. If a city is built over a fault line, it is liable to be hit by an earthquake which will result in the death of many of its citizens. All of these outcomes could be stopped by God, one way or another; but if God did regularly act to frustrate the lawful train of events, then we would have no responsibility for our acts and no means to learn about what sensible and what was foolish.

Moreover, we would have a disincentive to learn about the world in which we live. This is because the more we understood about the world, the more it would be equitable for us to take responsibility for our actions; and this would mean that we could not expect God to protect us from our own ignorance: as a parent acts to protect an infant from its lack of understanding of its environment, and the implications of its actions.It would then be very tempting to choose to remain ignorant, so as to be able to rely on God's benevolence: which would ensure that we never came to any harm whatever we did; no matter how irresponsible, reckless or foolish our actions.

This would condemn us to perpetual infancy and immaturity, and to an absolute dependency on God as parent, and would frustrate us from ever coming to know God as friend. This is why God does not regularly subvert the natural order of things so as to protect us from our folly or even from our ignorance.

That's a pretty story you've contrived to tell, Theo; but it has one gaping hole in it. As I understand it you still claim that in Heaven, and then in the New World of the Resurrection, there will be no suffering – and it seems that you attribute this to God behaving in exactly the way which you say God simply must not behave if we are going to be mature ethical beings, worthy of communion with God! This is an arrant nonsense! You always stress how axiomatic systems must be self-consistent and tell me that my ideas are incoherent; and here you are putting forward an account which has a huge contradiction at its very core!

I can see why you'd think this, Nyx, but in fact you are mistaken. What I am claiming is that in order for us to learn what good and evil are – to become ethically competent – it is necessary for us to exist in a world with "moral hazard", in which God steps back and generally lets events take their course according to physical law. However, once we have enough experience to understand the idea of "right and wrong", and to accept – of our own judgement – the basic premise that we ought to be virtuous, and hence come to "hunger and thirst for righteousness";[2] then the reason for God to step back ends.

Moreover, it is also entirely possible that what happens in the world of the resurrection isn't so much that God intervenes continually so as to stop every misfortune, as that we ourselves gain sufficient insight and power as to do this for ourselves. After all, we are promised that we will "come to share in the divine nature."[3] Once their education is complete a student graduates and becomes themselves a practitioner of the discipline they have been studying.

---

2   Mat 5:6.
3   2Pet 1:4.

I concede that there's some sense in your account, Theo, though I'm not convinced: the atrocities that abound in this world seem to me far more than can be accommodated in your scheme.

There is another point that I must raise. According to you everything is accountable to God, and so God is directly and solely responsible for everything that is wrong about human beings – every act of every tyrant and psychopath – and about the hostile environment in which we have to try to survive.

It follows that humans have nothing to learn from their experience because they are incapable of learning autonomously. Everything is the outworking of a programme which is pre-determined by God, and there is no place for human free-will, or autonomy, or whatever you want to call it! The whole situation goes beyond the mere human experience of suffering: it is a deep matter of justice.

Hold on, Nyx. This is a complex accusation. I must first respond by asking you whether you believe any human being – and in particular yourself – is in any way responsible for their actions? I think you do believe this is the case, because I have a strong idea that you blame yourself for any number of things: and mostly things that are really other people's fault, not yours.

Now, whatever "personal responsibility" means (and this isn't as simple an idea as it might seem) either you agree with me that it is real, in which case we also agree that it cannot be correct to blame God for everything; or else you disagree with me. In the latter case you must either believe that God is real and is morally repugnant, or else that God is not real and the Universe is itself somehow morally repugnant. You now either have to show how God could be morally repugnant, given that God is the Greatest Conceivable Being; or else show what "moral repugnance" means without any reference to God.

The first task is deeply problematic as "being morally repugnant" would compromise God's necessary perfection: you would be claiming that "injustice" is somehow greater than "justice", when justice is a positive thing whereas injustice is merely a lack of justice – but this is absurd. The second task is equally problematic; for as soon as you make any reference to objective standards of justice (and you have done this) I shall observe that objective justice is exactly what I mean by God, and that you cannot believe in objective justice and disbelieve in God.

The only way out of this conundrum is to adopt a Nihilist position; but in that case one has nothing to complain about, as justice is then no more that a delusion and suffering is of no significance whatsoever – which invalidates your complaint at its very root. Once cannot sensibly answer a heart-felt cry for vindication with the response "there ain't no justice!"

The fact is that the very idea of "justice" is bound up with the idea of God. It is not bound up with the idea of "god" in the polytheistic sense of that word, of course. The gods of every polytheistic religion I know are supposed to be tyrannical, or at best whimsical agents; but the God of the Bible (though sometimes portrayed in a similar light, especially in myths found in the oldest texts) is clearly stated to be just, benevolent and merciful: even in those same most ancient documents.

Alright, Theo, let me grant you this for the sake of the argument; let us assume that God is real, and is responsible for this world as we find it, and also that God is just. How is there any room for human autonomy in the scheme of things? What would "autonomy" mean? Why would it matter? How does its existence excuse God from direct and absolute culpability for every tragedy, atrocity and calamity that has ever taken place and will ever take place in the future? It seems to me that your position is just as self-contradictory as you claim mine to be.

Whereas I have the difficulty of showing how I can make sense of the claim that the world is full of injustice without recourse to the notion of absolute justice, which you claim is simply God in disguise; you have the difficulty of showing how God can be just, when God's creative act is full of injustice.

You claim (and I agree that this makes some kind of sense) that the explanation hinges on "human autonomy" but you have given no account of what this means – or that it even exists! It seems to me that if God is "necessary being" then everything that depends on God must be necessary too and there is no room for any kind of autonomy.

I understand your point, Nxy. Moreover I agree that it is an important one. Philosophers have been arguing about "Free-Will" for a very long time, and have come to no definite conclusion about the matter. However I think a few things can be said which are relevant and helpful.

The first is that this isn't really about God. The same problem exits on a purely materialistic view of the world. In as far as the world is governed by physical laws, it would seem to follow that human beings have no real choice: their every act being governed and determined by the outworking of those laws – however those laws come to be whatever they are, and whether or not they should be attributed to the agency of God.

In fact this was one of the big problems that theologians and philosopher's had with Newton's physics. It seemed to turn the Cosmos into a complex piece of clock-work, and to remove any semblance of spontaneity, choice and freedom from reality. Subsequently we have come to understand the difference between "causality" – which the Newtonian or Einsteinian world view depends upon – and "determinism" – which is not implied in or by any form of Classical Physics.

Moreover the advent of Quantum Mechanics has thrown a spanner into the Newtonian mechanism by making it seem that at the most basic level of reality every event is entirely spontaneous, whimsical and uncaused. Quantum indeterminacy doesn't explain "free-will" any more than does Classical indeterminacy; but any form of indeterminacy makes room for something other than absolute necessity.

The second point is that autonomy is about personal moral responsibility more than about "freedom to choose". Even if we are not in any sense "free to choose", we are still morally responsible for our actions. This is because the causation of our acts is two-fold. In general our acts are partly elicited by our past and present experience and environment: "external factors"; and partly by our dispositions, character, mood, expectations, theories, prejudices, habits, beliefs and so on: "internal factors". To the extent that our acts are explicable in terms of "internal factors", then we are responsible for them – and can expect to be praised (and perhaps rewarded) for them if those acts were in accord with justice, and to be blamed (and perhaps punished) for them if they were contrary to justice.

The fact that "we couldn't have acted differently" is no excuse. The hope is that the experience of praise (and reward) will reinforce wholesome, constructive and virtuous dispositions and habits and that the experience of blame (and punishment) will erode harmful, destructive and vicious dispositions and habits. Hence it is possible to clearly conceive of moral education even in a purely deterministic universe. All that is needed is for an expert educator to reward virtue and punish vice.

"Free-will" doesn't come into it at all. Indeed, it seems to me that one only needs to believe in "free-will" if one wants to try to rationalise vengeance or retribution: the idea that someone "deserves to suffer simply because they have done wrong," rather than that "we owe it to the perpetrator of injustice to make them suffer appropriately: for their own benefit, betterment, reformation and healing."

The third point is that what we call "free-will" or "autonomy" may in fact be an obscure aspect of determinism. It is just about possible that every event (not just human "choices") has two kinds of cause, namely a temporal or original cause and a counter-temporal or final cause. What I mean is that as well as an event coming to be because of previous events it may also come to be because of future events. In other words, one can only make full sense of what is happing now by taking into account what will happen in the future, and not just what happened in the past.

Our notion of "free-will" may be a mistaking of the fact that we have no knowledge of the future (and so no ability to explain the present in terms of the future) as evidence that there is a mysterious agency at work in the present apart from physical law: this agency being "freewill".[4]

If this is true, a Monotheist will immediately realise that it resolves the age-old debate about grace versus free-will; for the "pull of the future" on present events would be at least a good part of both what one calls "free-will" and "grace". The future, after all, is supposed to be an entire vindication of justice: which is the

---

4   UPSY

desire of any properly rational being – and so congruent with "free-will"; and also God's purpose for every rational being – and so congruent with "actual grace".

This seems like entrapment, to me Theo. God has entrapped us into loving Him by our very imperfect design. So there is no free will, and no escape from His grasp! What is the point of having the knowledge of what is good and evil when you are trapped to do only one thing: enter communion with God? I choose to be Lucifer!

How are you entrapped, Nyxos, and how come that if you are somehow entrapped you feel free to reject God? You say that there is no free-will and then immediately claim to exercise it! This is self-contradictary. If there is no free-will and no escape from God's grasp, then how come there are so many Atheists and God-haters out there? The empirical evidence is overwhelmingly against you.

It is seems obvious that we are not trapped to do one thing; but if you are right, then it would seem that you are trapped by God into rejecting God. How does that make sense? You seem to be saying that you think that God has specifically created you so that you are bound to reject God without you having any say in the matter. I suppose that John Calvin would agree with you, but I don't – and neither does the Catholic and Orthodox tradition.

We don't at present have a clear knowledge of what is good, or of what is the right thing to do: hence we do what is wrong all too often – often from decent motives. Being in communion with God is nothing other than coming to know with certainty what is good, and coming to see clearly what is beautiful; being loved and accepted without reservation; and having complete security and peace and joy. It means being fulfilled, and becoming the very best version of yourself that is possible.

In Nietzschian terms this is to become ones congruent Superman. In Catholic terms it is to become a saint and to "participate in the divine nature."[3] This is what, it seems to me, you desire; and yet you insist on rejecting what the Catholic Faith offers not as "fake, but nice if it were true," but rather as objectionable in character – which makes no sense.

If God was only masquerading as Being, Justice, Beauty and Truth – the plethora of what is Good; and God's business was to get us to acknowledge His nature as being Good, when it wasn't so; and if God had made us so that we could do nothing other than make that acknowledgement; then that would definitely be "entrapment". However, God is identical with that which is actually Good; so this possibility does not arise. You must remember at all times that we are talking here of God and not "a god".

Contrariwise, this is akin to the Devil's business. The Devil does masquerade as being just, beautiful and a teller-or-truth; and he does seem keen to get people to acknowledge his expertise and character in such matters. It is the Devil who tries to entrap us by pandering to our desires for absolute independence (which is a contradiction in terms) and to our conceit or hubris and also, sometimes, by feeding our feelings of resentment, desperation, bitterness, anger and disillusionment.

What you mean is that it seems to you that I, as a Monotheist, have to believe human autonomy a sham, whereas you can believe it to be real. Well in fact I don't believe that human autonomy is a sham. You must therefore show that first, my position requires me to believe that it is a sham; and second, that such a belief would be wrong if it were to be forced on me.

Now, I tend to agree with this second part. The notion of autonomy strikes me as being very important: both in itself, and also as a necessary part of any resolution of "the problem of suffering"; but for me this is not a foregone conclusion, because I admit that I am not clear as to what is meant by free-will or autonomy, or as to why this notion is as important as I believe it to be.

I acknowledge that in some sense God as "Necessary Being" can only give rise to "what is necessary"; but this is just a theological way of saying that a reality governed by physical law has to be exactly what it is – unless there is some "random" or "whimsical" element, as the conventional interpretation of Quantum Mechanics suggests. Hence whatever is meant by autonomy or free-will must be accommodated somehow by "necessity" (and, perhaps "randomness" or "whimsy") and this is the case whether or not one explicitly speaks of the basic fact of reality as being God.

What I would very much like to do is to explore with you what free-will or autonomy can mean in the context of there being a lawful backdrop to existence: how human beings can be autonomous given their genetic inheritance, the laws of physics and the actual facts of their environment and experiences. Are you willing to do this?

Perhaps, Theo, perhaps; but there is another issue which is related to this and perhaps if we consider this the matter may be resolved.

What is that, Nyx?

Well, it seems to me that some of my problems with your perspective may arise from the way in which you seem to anthropomorphise God. If you would just admit that God is an impersonal force or principle: simply "the necessity that makes possibility actual," then I might have no alternative but to admit that such must be the case, and to give in and become a Monotheist – but without really changing my views at all.

Well I can't do that Nyx; though I do take your point. In particular, I think that many people who profess belief in God do not really believe in God at all, but rather in some anthropomorphic "god" which they then mistake for God. "A stern father-figure in the sky who keeps a beady eye on us every moment of our lives, with a view to punishing us for our each sin and failing," is so far from what God is in fact as to be dismissed as an idol. Indeed, any understanding of God which attributes human characteristics to God (except in an analogous way) is absolutely wrong.

When "God's wrath" or "God's hatred of sin" is referred to in the Bible, this doesn't mean that God is capable of anger, or is motivated to seek vengeance. That doesn't make any sense at all. These phrases signify that sin – simply because of what sin is – has inescapable negative consequences for the sinner, and often other folk also. These consequences are being poetically spoken of as the extrinsic punishment of an angry judge, rather than as the intrinsic consequences of the sinful actions, attitudes or dispositions themselves. To take such poetry at face value is to mistake the analogy for what it is, and to fall into grave error which is bound to lead to intellectual disaster. The Bible (especially the Old Testament) very often speaks of God analogically: projecting onto God motives and actions which would make some sense if God was quasi-human, but which are in fact poetic transformations of what is actually the case.

On occasion God is said to "harden the heart" of a sinner. This seems to mean that God sets out to make that sinner persist in their sin so that they have no chance to repent, and be forgiven, and escape the consequences of their error. What it really means is that they did not in fact repent, and so did not in fact escape the consequences of their sin. The Bible likes to attribute everything that happens directly to God's agency – even when the truth of the matter is that human autonomy had a considerable part to play in the affair.

This is because the Bible authors wants to make it clear that human autonomy cannot frustrate God's providence, and that our freedom and foolishness cannot obstruct God from vindicating righteousness in the end. God is in charge, and all will be well, no matter how much we act so as to seem to disrupt God's benevolent purposes for us.

Now I said that I couldn't go along with your suggestion that I should de-anthropomorphise God. Let me explain what I mean. First, I hope that I have made it abundantly clear that I do not actually anthropomorphise God – except, perhaps, in an occasional lapse of thought. Hence I have no need to do any de-anthropomorphising. Second, I must insist that although God is only remotely like a human being (and one must remember that humans are supposed to be created "in God's image"[5] and are invited to "share in the divine nature"[3] – and so cannot

5   Gen 1:26-27.

be entirely different from God) God is not less than human; but much more than human. This means that God is not a person, but rather transpersonal: God is three-persons-in-community and I cannot down-play this. Third, I believe that God has made Himself human and so is guilty of objective anthropomorphism.

The Catholic doctrine of the tri-personal constitution of God is of extreme importance for two reasons. First, if God were not personal (whatever "personal" means, exactly) how could persons come to be from out of God? God must contain within the eternal divine reality every excellence and substantive aspect of temporal existence. Given that you and I are persons, God's reality must encompass what it is to be personal. Hence God must at least be a person; but more plausibly much more than a person. Second, if God were only a single person, then God would not be able to be love in actuality, as we are told is the case by St John;[6] but only be loving in potentiality, as is the case in the Muslim view of Allah: who is supposed to be loving towards creatures, but apart from creatures has no object to love and so cannot be a lover or know love in and of the divine reality.

This would be a huge defect compared to what is conceivable, so it is not surprising that God reveals Himselves to be a community of persons, bound together by eros. For love (in all its flavours and variants) to be acknowledged as of pre-eminent importance, one has to acknowledge that "God is love"[4] or, if you like, "Love is God" and this necessitates God as being personal – and to be more than a single person.

The Catholic doctrine of the Incarnation is also of profound importance, for without it all we would have of and from God is "words" and "teachings". Now such things are not worthless; but they pale into insignificance beside the fact that God really became one of us as a particular man in history, and experienced our futility and suffering, and died: so as to show – not just tell – us what "being God" means in human terms; and to show – not just tell – us that God is absolutely committed to humanity without any hint of conditionality.

---

6   1Jn 4:8.

You miss my point, Theo. What is free-will, if the choice is singular; if all we can choose is "fellowship with God in the end," and nothing else? This seems to invalidate the answer you gave to the problem of suffering: that we are here to learn a lesson. What is the value of this lesson, when we don't get to apply it freely to obtain the things we want? Why create an autonomous being and damn it to a singular fate? It seems to me that religion is based on the notion that we are born into this world to be groomed for an eternal existence with God. That makes God heinous and repulsive doesn't it?

I do understand, Nyxos and I shall address each of these points one at a time.

You ask: "What is free-will, if the choice is singular; if all we can choose is ;fellowship with God in the end,' and nothing else?"

I reply, first: autonomy is not about there being real alternatives of outcome (I can't see how this could be, in any case; but I may be wrong about that: it's not something that I insist on) but about what happens being a spontaneous out-flowing of ones own constitution and character, rather than resulting from external injunctions, pressure, or constraints.

Second: fellowship with God encompasses all that anyone could rationally desire, so there is no need for any alternative.

Third: there is a multitude of modes, styles or ways in which a soul can enter "fellowship with God", depending on the character of the soul in question. God is unitary, true, and so is the one same identical reality for every soul; but souls themselves differ, and so must the relationship between each soul and God, in accordance with the particularity of that soul. God provides for each soul what is specifically beneficial for and pertinent to that soul, while not holding back on any aspect of the entirety of the divine being.

You ask: "What is the value of this lesson, when we don't get to apply it freely to obtain the things we want?"

I reply, first: an important part of our education in this here-and-now is finding out what we need rather than what we want. When our souls are truly healthy (when we are wise and enlightened) there is no difference between what we need and what we want, and we can be content and happy without any compromise: we will certainly have everything that we want.

Second: I suspect and conjecture (but do not assert and insist) that the reason for our present education is that the future world beyond death will be constituted by God so that it also could go wrong if we abused our autonomy. Hence it is important that before we enter into the resurrection life we are all thoroughly virtuous and entirely disinclined to do anything that would disrupt our own well-being or that of anyone else.

You ask: "Why create an autonomous being and damn it to a singular fate?"

I reply, first: I do not know why God creates autonomous beings – unless it is simply that God simply can't do otherwise. After all, if God is omniscient and omnipotent how can God avoid making real every thing that is conceivable?

Second: if there were to be a singular fate for every autonomous being, this wouldn't necessarily be any kind of damnation. Third: I have already explained that any such singular fate is certain to be differentiated in keeping with the varied character of individual souls.

You ask: "It seems to me that religion is based on the notion that we are born into this world to be groomed for an eternal existence with God. That makes God heinous and repulsive doesn't it?"

I reply, first: this is not the case of all religions. Ancient Judaism had no clear idea of an eternal existence with God after death. Buddhism has the idea that the best hope for the personal soul is that it is entirely dissipated and looses all individuation and autonomy. I can't speak for Taoism, Hinduism, Shinto, Jainism or Zoroastrianism…

Second: "grooming" nowadays has a nasty sense attached to it, but here you are really using it to signify training as opposed to education. This is an important distinction. It can be understood to be the basic difference between bad religion and good religion. Bad religion is all about guilt, condemnation, conformity, subjugation and unthinking obedience: "grooming", if you insist. Good religion is all about joy, forgiveness, self-discipline, self-discovery, self-fulfilment, enlightenment, spontaneity, freedom, justice, peace and integrity.

Third: God is in no way malicious or repulsive. God has nothing to gain from us and has no motive to exploit or abuse us in any way. God's only business with and in us is to uplift each one of us to the perfection, excellence and beauty of which we are capable.

That's all well and good, Theo, but what you spell out is still a singular fate. There is no way to opt out, or to become gods ourselves. I did not agree to sign up for this life, or this "education" that I am supposed to get from it. Nor did I ask Jesus to die for my sins – after all, I believe in personal responsibility! A point in a circle is no more than a point in circle regardless of its unique coordinates! God may love me, but I don't love Him!

My dear Nyxos, you are right that this fate is singular; but you are wrong about what that means. I have made it clear that there are as many ways of "being a saint" as there are human beings – so the idea that this singularity implies uniformity, or the destruction of personality, is ruled out. That is a Buddhist idea, not one that has any place in Judeo-Christianity!

Your idea of humans becoming "gods" is either the same as the Catholic idea that humans can become "saints" and "share in the divine nature"[3], or is very much less than this idea. A god can be nothing like as powerful or glorious as is God, and for human beings to "come to share in the divine nature"[3] is a much greater destiny than "becoming gods". A god – as exemplified in Hindu, Norse or Egyptian mythology –

is always an up-graded human being, complete with foibles and limitations. God is not like that. We are created in God's image,[2] in as far as we are rational beings, and are conscious and have the potentiality for enlightenment and uplifting (by means of autonomous education) so as to share in the One divine nature[3] which is the foundation all that exists: complete Justice, unconditional Love, absolute Being and entirely realised Potency – which terms are more or less synonyms.

Saints are not "points in a circle". The divine nature does not have parts in the sense that a circle is made up of distinguishable points. The divine nature is Justice: and this is a gestalt or extensive property. It cannot be sub-divided or shared out. It is unitary and inclusive of all that is good, right and proper. Every saint possesses this wholly and entirely; but manifests it in a different way – in accord with their particular personality. Your idea of humans becoming gods is more in keeping with "points in a circle", where each point would be a god and the circle the pantheon.

Of course you didn't "sign up" for any of this. Apart from your creation you did not exist and had no power to either accept or reject the prospect of your creation. That initiative inevitably belongs with God alone: by the nature of the case, and is no cause for complaint. You can either accept the gift of life and pursue its meaning on to salvation, enlightenment, joy and glory; or you can angrily reject it and fade into the darkness. That is your choice; but only a perverse nature could opt for the second.

It is not unjust for God to grant life on the risk that the recipient of this free-gift will grumpily object to its own existence: that is a matter for individual created beings, not their benevolent Creator. I know that the lives that we have to lead are sometimes tough and troublesome, and that you have had a particularly rough deal; but in the end all we have is this choice: life, to make of it what we are able; and death, which makes nothing out of us. Choose life!

Of course you didn't ask Jesus to die for your sins! He didn't have to be asked. Just as God had to take the initiative in making you from nothing, God had to take the initiative in redeeming you from the fate of reverting to nothing. There are so many

reasons for God becoming man and dying as a man that one
can only wonder at God's providential love and wisdom.

As for "personal responsibility" this is a two-edged sword.
Yes, we each are responsible for our actions and their outcomes;
but we are not capable of bearing that burden unaided. Sometimes
very small decisions (even made in all innocence) can have
horrendous consequences. We can't undo these things or put right
their consequences (and they may not even been our "fault")
but we can hand the situation over to God, asking for forgiveness
for whatever element of blame is rightly lodged with us.

You and I cannot put the world to rights. All we can do is
strive our best to act justly, and to make up for all those failings of
which we become aware. Anyone who holds on to feelings
of guilt or shame (whether justified or unjustified) will eventually
be destroyed by them. This is why the sacrament of Confession
(or Penance) is so important to Catholics: it enables the shame
of past wrongful acts to be absolved – the chains that bind us to
those acts be broken. God's love of you is not conditional on you
loving God; but it is ordered towards you coming to love God:
for in that love lies your hope of salvation and joy.

Alright, let it rest Theo; but what about the status of other
religions? You have made no mention of that issue: only of your
supposedly Catholic ideas about life death and resurrection.
I've nothing against the idea of rebirth, or the idea that
we maybe able to escape the cycle; nor am I opposed to idea
of a yet undiscovered dimension to human existence.

The status of other religions is a large and complex one, Nyxos.
Judaism stands apart in a category of its own, as being God's
particular instrument of preparation for the life, passion, death,
resurrection and ascension of Jesus.

Without going into lots of details, I'd say that there is some
good stuff in most other religions. Sometimes there is lots of good
stuff there. Some of this good stuff can be attributed to human
wisdom, and some of it to divine inspiration. St Paul tells us that

God does not leave Himself "without witnesses"[7] anywhere and also that the basis of righteousness is to be found in the heart of every human being. He also tells us that "whoever would draw near to God must believe that He exists and that He rewards those who seek him,"[8] Jesus first presented this idea by saying: "Blessed are those who hunger and thirst for righteousness: for they shall be satisfied."[9]

Catholicism is the best medium for salvation, as it presents the truth of the matter in the most explicit and coherent way, and also offers the sacraments as great helps towards progress in the spiritual and ethical life.

The idea of reincarnation has its roots in a pretty horrid philosophy. It is more about finding an easy answer to the problem of suffering than anything else. The Catholic idea of being born "anew", or "from above"[10] is quite different. This is something that can happen here-and-now as part of the single mortal life one has. It is the moment when a person accepts that living in isolation from God (that is, in sin) is doing them no good and they turn from that life-trajectory (which leads only to darkness and death) and adopt a different path. This moment is ratified and expressed in sacramental baptism with water.

The "undiscovered dimension to human existence" is, of course exactly what Catholicism is all about!

Well that's given me a great deal to think about, Theo. I think that is enough for today, don't you?

Yes, Nyxos, I agree with you. I look forward to resuming this discussion at a later date.

---

7   Acts 14:17.
8   Heb 11:6. RSV
9   Mat 5:6. RSV
10 Jn 3:3-7. 1Pet 1:23.

Primon: a Platonic dialogue

Ah, there you are, Pharsea. I'd been hoping to catch you. I wanted to ask you about the article you've just written about the Incarnation. I think I understand the Protestant version of the doctrine, and don't like it. I don't think I fully understand the Catholic version yet.

Dear Primon, it is good to see you, as always. I suppose that you are intent on asking lots of questions. Don't expect to "fully" understand any doctrine! I'm pretty sure that I don't. In any event, I expect that your questions will direct me to explore issues that I hadn't even noticed before.

You won't get around me as easily as that, Pharsea!

You can't blame me for trying, dear boy! It is true that I find our discussions valuable and enlightening, and I am keen to give you every incentive to continue them!

Enough then! The point is that I'm not sure that what you have written totally makes sense to me. Some of what you write suggest that there were lots of ways God could have acted in some sense, as far as being loving to us and giving us a good shot of getting to heaven, but He chose to act in a certain way which was the "best way" on some metric; as of course He must, in another sense.

Exactly so. Thomas Aquinas tells us that for the God-Man to shed a single tear would have been adequate recompense for all the sins of humanity. I find that a wonderful idea. Especially given the profligate way in which Jesus cried over Jerusalem and how he groaned in agony over the death of his beloved Lazarus.

But seriously, Pharsea, why did God become Man?

I'm not sure that I'll be able to offer a satisfactory answer to your question, Primon. If you find that I can, then let us rejoice together and still question whether what we are content with should really satisfy our hearts. If you find that I cannot, then let us strive together to track down as best we may the prize that as yet evades us.

That sounds fine to me.

Good. Then, as best I see it, this question is all to do with God's respect for mankind and the fact that He wanted to be our friend, not just our master. He wanted to be able to see things from our point of view and to gain an understanding of suffering.

Both these arguments seem wrong, Pharsea. If God were omniscient, He could see things from any view He wanted and He would understand everything anyway!

Yes and no. There is theoretical knowledge on the one hand and experiential knowledge on the other. It is one thing for an observer to claim to account for and describe every aspect of someone else's experience. It is quite another for them to claim that they have experienced something similar themselves.

I suppose so, but why does this matter?

Well, Primon, consider a psychiatrist who is an expert on Depression but has never been depressed herself. She may know all the biochemistry and psychology and physiology, and be able to diagnose depression very accurately – and also effectively cure it: but unless she has herself been depressed she cannot say that she understands what it is to be depressed.

But why does this matter, if she has the skill and knowledge to help her patient?

Of course, as a professional it doesn't. It is supremely unimportant as to whether she knows what it is to be depressed. All that matters is whether she can help someone who is depressed to become not depressed any more! But God doesn't want to have a professional relationship with us, God wants to be our friend.

Well enough, Pharsea, but what's to stop God from being our friend?

God cannot suffer or indeed experience in HimSelves any kind of change. While God knows what change and suffering are, objectively, God has no personal experience of either. God doesn't need to have any such experience: either for His own good or even in order to help us; but, God wanted to totally identify with us. He wanted to make it clear that He does understand just what it is to be human and to change and to have passions and to be tempted and to be betrayed and to suffer and to die. He chose to experience all these things in Jesus. Hence, the writer of the Epistle to the Hebrews says that Jesus is a compassionate High Priest who can sympathize with us in our weakness.

So you're saying that without the Incarnation, Man and God don't have enough in common to be friends?

Yes, Primon: exactly so. God wanted to "muck in with us" rather than just observe and issue orders. Also, it is only because of the Incarnation that we can sensibly pray along the lines: "You know what it's like, Lord: I can't put it into words, but I know that You've been through something along the same lines and that You feel for me in this situation." Neither a Jew nor a Muslim can pray like this.

God could help us as much as He likes – if this is what you mean by "mucking in with us" – without having to choose between "just observing and issuing orders" and "becoming human."

Of course. But God isn't ever about what He could do, but about extravagance, over-brimming generosity and enthusiasm. God is infinite and never does anything by half measures. If there is something that He could do, then He'll do it: because He has infinite resources and infinite time and infinite patience. Hence, I am rather inclined to the view (along with Origen, who was excommunicated after his death for holding it!) that most people are saved, one way or another, in the end.

So you're saying, Pharsea, that it's wrong to understand the incarnation in terms of what God had to do, but instead marvel at what in fact He chose to do?

Yes, you have it. God wanted to show us directly what it is to be good, rather than just to use some intermediary: a prophet or holy book.

This seems reasonable, but if some other perfectly human person – such as Mary – is already good, there is no need for someone else who is God Himself, to set us an example.

There are degrees of independence from God, Primon. Mary was incapable of sinning, because She was constrained by God's continual support and "hand holding" from ever making a wrong decision. Also, She was protected from many assaults on Her integrity by God's providence. This is not a viable plan for dealing with every human being. It was certainly not the case for Her Divine Son!

But I also think that you are saying there is more to the Incarnation than God setting us an example, Pharsea. It's the rest of the package that really bothers me.

Yes, Primon, there is more to the Incarnation than just an education programme! God also wanted to identify and ally with us absolutely in the face of the worst that sin and the Devil could throw at Him.

I'm not sure how becoming human comes into this, Pharsea. Couldn't "sin and the Devil throw anything at Him" if he weren't human?

Of course not. That is part of my point! He became man precisely so that they could! Apart from the Incarnation, nothing could harm God. Nevertheless, something had to be done about the awkward fact that the Cosmos – God's Work of Art – needed remedial action.

If God is perfect anyway, what does it mean for sin to throw anything at Jesus? Wasn't it all rather a sham?

The fact that Jesus was not just The Ideal Man, but God, made temptation worse for Him. We generally give in before temptation gets too hard to handle – unless circumstances rescue us. Jesus simply was incapable of giving in to temptation, but He didn't defeat temptation by using His Divine Omniscience to inform his rational soul with episteme. Rather He simply chose to up the stakes, bid by bid. As Satan deployed more and more persuasive arguments, Our Lord called upon more and more of His Divine Wisdom to counter them: but only just enough to do so. In this way, every temptation seemed to be exquisitely irresistible while in fact it was just barely resisted. Hence, Jesus came to know first hand more about what temptation feels like than any of us can begin to imagine.

All right, Pharsea, but what did you mean by saying that God "wanted to identify and ally with us"?

Just by becoming Man, God tore up the "bill of divorce" that Adam and Eve had initialled on our behalf at the beginning of the human race. Only God-made-Man could do this. No human being – even if sinless and of superb virtue and holiness could do this.

But this is part of the point, Pharsea. If God can do it, he can do it without being human. If a perfect human can do it, then again it does not need God to become human.

You are correct, Primon, but your syllogism misses the point. The truth is that no perfect human could do it. While God could do it without becoming human, He chose to do it by becoming human because it was – in His judgement – the very best way of doing it.

Are you sure about this, Pharsea? This seems to me to be crucial! If God is able to forgive us without the Incarnation, why did He bother with the whole messy rigmarole?

God could always let us off for our wickednesses large and small. Of course, He always did do so, in practice: but – more than this – He wanted to abolish the power of sin per se.

I always heard He was only allowed to let people off in the Old Testament because of Jesus. Because the Incarnation was a timeless event, it does not matter whether sin came before or afterwards, the fact that Jesus abolished the power of sin, was once for all time.

You really shouldn't pay so much attention to idle gossip, my friend! The idea that God "was not allowed" to do something is obviously silly. I am sure that you know this and can also see why it is silly.

I suppose you're right, Pharsea: but about this "abolishing the power of sin": if God can do it, why did He need to become human to do so? Also, when you say that Jesus "defeated the power of sin" in some sense, I am not sure in what sense this is true. Sin holds power over plenty of people's lives and seems rampant in the world.

As to "why did God had to become human," I have already answered this: He didn't have to from necessity, but chose to because it was the best way for us. As to in what sense Jesus "defeated the power of sin," He did so in denying us any excuse for thinking that "we are not good enough" for God. This idea keeps many people back from God. By His Incarnation, God demonstrates that His love and forgiveness and offer of healing and wholeness and holiness is free and without precondition. While you are right that, sadly: "sin holds power over plenty of people's lives and seems rampant in the world," none of us have any excuse not to turn to God for forgiveness and healing and wholeness. We can have total confidence that He is benevolent and not vengeful.

But Protestants say that God hates sin and that His sense of justice impels him to take vengeance. Isn't this part of Catholic teaching?

Bless my soul, Primon, certainly not! Of course God hates sin: He sees injustice in all its forms for exactly what it is, and it is never attractive. However, the idea that He is vindictive and vengeful is a wrong and debilitating view that came out of a twisted interpretation of both the Natural and Mosaic Laws.

So you're saying that the Jews got the wrong end of the stick?

Not quite. I'm saying that St Paul tells us that some Jews and some Gentiles twisted the Mosaic Code and the Natural Law from being guides and reminders of Justice into sentences of guilt, and in doing so lost all reasonable hope of salvation.

So you don't think that God punishes wickedness, Pharsea?

It is certainly true that "the wages of sin is death": that injustice rebounds on the evil-doer and that this is only right and proper; but God's wish is only for the repentance of the sinner so that they can be forgiven and saved from the natural consequences of their own actions.

It still seems to me that repentance and a request of God to help remove the sin is necessary.

Yes, Primon, always; but not because of some arbitrary rule: rather because of the nature of the case. Without repentance, nothing can be done to start the healing process and unless the soul asks God for help, God will not impose a cure.

So it's like a cancer patient committing himself to giving up smoking and signing a "consent to treatment" contract?

Yes, Primon, except that God doesn't just wait for the sinner to ask for help, but continually pesters and badgers and encourages him to do so. Moreover, God also undertakes to help and support the sinner in his programme of conversion of life that he freely undertakes.

So would repentance and then a request to God that he help purify us from sin not be possible without the Incarnation?

No! This was always possible under the Mosaic Covenant, no more and no less than under the earlier covenants made with Noah and Abraham! By His Incarnation, God acted to make things easier for us, to give us more encouragement and incentive: to make us bolder in seeking His love and forgiveness and help.

You make God sound like a weak-willed parent colluding with an incorrigible child!

Well, I hope it's not quite like that, Primon, but certainly God does want to entice us towards righteousness at any cost and by using any technique that He can call to his disposal!

This is all very flattering, I suppose!

That's as maybe. What is certainly true is that God wanted to give to us rights and a certain dignity. He wanted to make us "co-heirs with Christ", so that we would not have to keep on asking for special consideration and mercy. In practice, of course, we still pray for God's mercy: mostly I think because we can't really believe what Jesus has in fact done for us!

I'm still not sure of precisely what He has in fact done that would mean we do not need to pray for such things.

He has written us a blank cheque, if you like, Primon. We should accept this and stop asking him for further advances.

But I know that I am not perfect, Pharsea, and I believe I need to be perfected before I can enter the Kingdom.

You can enter the Kingdom without being perfect, Primon. Perfection relates to reaching the fullness of the Kingdom. Incidentally, what you say here shows that you are already very close to the Kingdom.

Has Jesus somehow already perfected me without me knowing it?

No, what a strange idea! But there is no doubt that if you simply allow God's grace to work in your life, by "relaxing and not fighting" and allowing yourself to be seduced in His strong but gentle arms, then you will be healed of all moral disorder and certainly become the best man that you can.

It seems then that I still should pray for God's help in the process, Pharsea as I can't do it alone.

Of course, my friend! But the praying that is required is not so much a request for God's help as an opening of your heart to God's gentle manipulation and caress.

But surely, I still should ask for God's forgiveness and mercy?

One sense of forgiveness and mercy relates to an escape from due punishment: being "let off", if you like. It is this that we really shouldn't pray for: because God has already let us off anything that there might have been to be let off from – if there was anything to be let off from in the first place, which I doubt! We don't need to ask for this except as a kind of inverted "thank you" that acknowledges what is already the case; however "mercy" can also mean kindness: being helpful towards another person. For example it is merciful to help someone in distress. In this sense, the Good Samaritan was merciful to the man who had been set upon by brigands. In this sense we should continually cry "Lord, have mercy!" confident that God will hear our prayers (which He himself inspires) and come to our aid!

Would I be unable to pray without the Incarnation, Pharsea? Would God be unable to listen?

Of course not!

That's well enough: but in which case, I don't see how the Incarnation helps.

The Incarnation should help you by giving you a greater confidence in prayer. It shows God's absolute commitment to the "Primon Perfection Project." After all, God invested His Life, Love and Death in it!

But I still think you're holding back on me, Pharsea. The Protestant story is all about God punishing Jesus instead of sinners. Does this have no counterpart in Catholic Theology?

No, not as such.

But you have written that the Protestant story is a distortion of Catholic theology, Pharsea. What did you mean by that?

The Catholic story is that Jesus offered an apology to God on our behalf, not that He offered Himself as a proxy or substitute, to be punished instead of us. Jesus' apology "made up for" the infinite offence that we mere mortals do towards God's infinite dignity every time we sin. It means that we can be proud before God: basking in the glory of our brother and friend and team-mate Jesus, not being forever ashamed and self-conscious of the ill that we have ourselves done.

It seems that you are saying the sin of a mere mortal is of infinite badness but the prefect life of a human is only of finite goodness in some balance.

Yes, Primon, this is exactly what I am saying. It's obvious if you think about it a little. The gravity of sin must take account of the infinite dignity of God, whereas the value of a perfect human life is at best finite.

Who decides these scales?

The scales don't have to be calibrated by anyone, the facts are just as they are. The scale is absolute.

I'm not so sure about that, Pharsea, but let it pass. How do you say that Jesus made this apology, then?

Jesus as God-Man was able to do a deed of superlative glory: as a man and for mankind, but raised to an infinite level of value and significance by the fact that it was a Divine Person who acted and experienced that act in the Human Nature He had assumed.

But what is the "deed", Pharsea, and why did it have to be done?

Jesus' deed was His whole Life, culminating in His death and resurrection. Jesus obeyed God, whereas Adam had disobeyed God. Jesus broke the bonds of sin by showing what was true about God and His attitude towards mankind. God didn't want Jesus to die, and took no pleasure in it. Objectively, Jesus' execution was the greatest sin of all time! It was offensive to God, not pleasing! However, God the Father was supremely pleased that God the Son stood by mankind even when He was betrayed by His friend and when leaders of mankind conspired to murder Him.

What do you mean by "breaking the bonds of sin"? I need something less figurative.

This is a reasonable request, Primon. I will do my best to explain.

Fair, enough. So: what are "the bonds of sin"?

They are the psychological isolation from God and the debilitating loss of hope which a knowledge of failure and self inadequacy brings with it.

How were these bonds, that you say exist, broken, Pharsea?

By Jesus showing that God will not accept any excuse as valid grounds for us being isolated and alienated from Him.

Could they have been broken in another way?

Perhaps, Primon: after all, who am I to say? It seems to me, however, that the Incarnation was a pretty neat answer to the problem situation!

What is the difference to us between them being broken and unbroken?

We have great grounds for hope!

What is the difference to God?

He has another seduction technique at His disposal!

I'm not convinced, Pharsea. It seems to me that if I run away when called upon, knowing that another human actually did respond to the call does not reduce my sense of shame. In some ways, it makes things worse for me: as it shows what is possible; whereas if I were a mouse, and incapable of controlling my urge to flee from fire, I might feel less ashamed!

Indeed, Primon, but there is a difference between subjective feelings of guilt and shame and any objective basis for such feelings. God's very purpose in becoming Man was to offer a cloak of dignity to sinners. To that extent, Luther was correct.

I can't believe my ears, you're actually saying that Luther was right about something?

Indeed I am, Primon! God does impute to sinners the merit of Christ. God does look at us in an especially kind manner saying:

> "Since it was one like you (though He is my Divine Son too) who honoured me (by honouring humanity: my master-work of love) and so repaired the necessary breach of trust that dogged our relationship; I will associated you with that honour and in turn I will honour you."

With this cloak of dignity being freely offered, there are no objective grounds for shame or guilt. It is just like the tender care shown by God for Adam and Eve as they were cast out of Eden to make their way in the world of ethical choices. God sewed His beloved children garments[1] to clothe their nakedness and to represent His approval of them and His commitment to them.

So what do you say is wrong with Luther's doctrine, then?

Where Luther got it wrong was that he said that this mere beginning of Justification (a change of status) was all that Justification was.

Whereas Catholic teaching is that Justification and Sanctification are much of a muchness, yes?

That's right, Primon. In Catholic Theology, even this initial recognition of the sinner as honourable by God is seen as a "credit advance" based on the fact that in the end the sinner will be a saint and honourable in their own right.

Another way of putting my difficulty is this. If I am pretty bad, but the best human around, I can say: "I might not be great, but You made me and given the way I was made, I have done pretty well," versus "here is someone who is made the same but managed way better," though Jesus wasn't made the same, so perhaps He doesn't count that way – whereas Mary would.

But as I've already said, Primon, Mary was given extraordinary prerogatives that I am sure could not be granted to all and sundry: but that is another story, I think!

---

1   Gen 3:21.

I think the issue of time is something you skip over, but it is consistent in your picture. Anything that happens at any specific time in this universe can not change God's behaviour either between, before or after the event – since God is outside time.

I skip over time, Primon, because it doesn't exist for God at all. I try to treat of God taking the Incarnation into account right from the start, so I don't keep on mentioning time.

Yes, well, it seems to me that the fact that some event happens once in the universe is enough for Him at all times. However, the effect on us, as humans within time can be different before and after the event. So Jesus' life, occurring within time, is about changing the attitude of humans to God, not the attitude of God towards humans.

That is beautifully put, Primon. I would never have come up with that simple summary, but I think that you've penetrated right to the heart of the matter there!

Well that was very interesting, Pharsea. I'm not sure if I'm any more convinced about the truth of what you're saying, but I suppose I have a clearer idea of how it all fits together.

I hope that this is true for both of us, dear friend, and thank you for making me think these issues through.

Bibliography

Films

A. Bird & J. McGovern "Priest"
(Miramax Films: 1994)
J. McCord "The Body"
(Avalanche Films: 2001)

Frequently referenced documents

FCD   L. Ott "Fundamental of Catholic Dogma"
(Tan; Rockford IL: 4th Ed 1974)
GOB   S.C. Lovatt "The Good of Being"
(CreateSpace; Seattle, WA: 2012)
UPSY   S.C. Lovatt "Understanding the PSyChE."
(CreateSpace; Seattle, WA: 2016)

Other documents referenced

Anon. "The Cloud of Unknowing" ed E. Underhill
(Stuart & Watkins; London 1970)
Anon. Sanhedrin 71a
http://www.dafyomi.co.il/sanhedrin/points/sn-ps-071.htm
Benedict XVI "Greeting to the Pastoral Council of
the Roman Parish of St Felicity and her children" (2007)
http://www.vatican.va/holy_father/benedict_xvi/
speeches/2007/march/documents/
hf_ben-xvi_spe_20070325_consiglio-pastorale_en.html
P. Davies "The Goldilocks Enigma"
(Penguin; London: 2006)
R. Dawkin "The God Delusion"
(Black Swan; London: 2007) p83

R. Descartes "Objections and Replies"
tr J. Bennett (2007) p12, 14, 15-16
http://www.earlymoderntexts.com/descor.pdf

D. Hulme "Dialogues Concerning Natural Religion"
in "The philosophical works of David Hume" vol 2
(Adam Black, William & Charles Tait; Edinburgh: 1826) p 498

I. Kant "The Critique of Pure Reason" IV (1781)
tr J.M.D. Meiklejohn

N. Kazantzakis "The Last Temptation of Christ"
(Simon Schuster Inc; New York: 1960)

S.C. Lovatt "A Sparrow Falls"
(CreateSpace; Seattle, WA: 2015)

S.C. Lovatt "In Reverence and Awe"
(CreateSpace; Seattle, WA: 2014)

S.C. Lovatt "Testaments"
(CreateSpace; Seattle, WA: 2016)

N. Malcolm "Anselm's Ontological Argument"
Phil. Rev. vol 69 #1 (1960) p41-62

P. Miller "The Anthropic Principle"
http://people.brandeis.edu/~pmiller/anthrop.html

Paul VI "Address to the Lombard College"
(Vatican; The Holy See: 7th Dec 1968)
Italian original: http://www.vatican.va/holy_father/
paul_vi/speeches/1968/december/documents/
hf_p-vi_spe_19681207_seminario-lombardo_it.html

Plato "Complete Works"
ed J.M. Cooper and D.S. Hutchinson
(Indianapolis, IN; Hackett: 1997).

K.R. Popper "The Logic of Scientific Discovery"
(Hutchinson; London: 1980)

Printed in Dunstable, United Kingdom